MODERN INVESTING

Gambling in Disguise

DAVID SCHNEIDER

THE
WRITINGALE
PUBLISHING

The Writingale Publishing also publishes its books in a variety of electronic formats. For more information about The Writingale Publishing products, visit our Web site at www.thewritingale.com.

ISBN-13:978-1537747262
ISBN-10:1537747266

Printed in the United States of America
First Edition: September 2016

TABLE OF CONTENTS

AUTHOR BIOGRAPHY

David Schneider

The author of the bestselling book *The 80/20 Investor* on Amazon in Wealth Management,[1] David Schneider bought his first stock in 1994 at age 18. Subsequently, he trained as a commercial banker in Germany and studied finance at London Metropolitan University. He concurrently worked as an Asset Management Trainee and continued as an Equity Research Associate in Tokyo, Japan, where he also studied at Waseda University School of Commerce.

From 2005, he co-founded two hedge funds with a Long/Short Equities strategy working in Tokyo and Singapore. He developed his bottom-up value approach for selecting investment opportunities and managing concentrated portfolios based on the 80/20 principle.

Since 2011 David has been an independent investor, entrepreneur, and writer. On his research blog and financial podcast—8020investingshow.com he covers topics including wealth management, financial markets with a critical and independent view, as well as finding investment opportunities around the world.

For performance references, please visit and subscribe to the 80/20 Model Portfolio at www.8020investingshow.com.

INTRODUCTION

When I purchased my first shares at 18, investing in stocks felt like playing a game. It was simple. The one with the most cash at the end won, right?

Just like gambling!

That's right—*gambling*. Thousands of economists and specialists may get upset at comparing investing to gambling. Yet, no one can deny that today's financial markets resemble giant casinos with players gambling with their own and other people's money. Before the recent Berkshire Hathaway annual meeting in 2016, Charlie Munger, the vice chairperson and Warren Buffett's sidekick, had nothing good to say about the current state of American finance. According to Munger, we have "a vast gambling culture, and people have made it respectable."[2] Gambling has become respectable in the name of growth—that thing which modern capitalism values above all else and which requires a constant flow of new money—most likely coming from you.

When talking to friends from non-financial backgrounds, I always notice their inner conflict with the topic of money, investing, and all things related to Wall Street. In the end, they give in and purchase financial products that are *en vogue* or touted particularly aggressively. Once a decision is made, it might feel exciting. They may reassure themselves that everybody is doing it, and experts recommend it until a rude awakening occurs, usually many months or years later. They are not aware that they just have committed to a gamble without a clue as to whether it will ever pay off. This is where the real suffering starts. The dotcom bubble in 2001, the subprime crisis in 2008, the Euro Crisis in 2011, and most recently, the confusion about the economic impact of Brexit—have all caused millions of people to lose money. Regular people, just like you. A brief look at the headlines should have made it clear how challenging this can be.

I remember one of the key lessons I learned from a high school history teacher: "You don't have to be an expert in all of the subjects you are studying. You only have to know enough on each topic, so that you can call bullshit on someone pretending to know more." When it comes to money and investing, most people simply ignore that crude, yet sound, advice. Often, people embarking on the perilous route of investing do so without a structured education in what investing is, and how it differs from gambling, particularly in financial markets. They don't understand the decision-making process involved and consistently underestimate the roles of psychology and chance. The majority of individual investors, who have no clue how to invest, are easy prey for unscrupulous market players. Common sense gets lost in a mess of financial theory and sales talk by so-called experts.

We all need to ask ourselves a simple question: do we need to play games in the first place?

Thank you for buying this book.

This book is for the novice investor, as well as the crowds of retail investors who feel they need to play "*The Money Game*," a term made famous in a book with the same title by author and investor George Goodman (a.k.a. columnist Adam Smith). There is a widespread need for education about money, investing and capitalistic systems, which teaches the basics, but also makes the student think critically and develop a healthy mistrust of an industry that encourages gambling where there is no need, and activity where inactivity would be the more prudent choice.

This book aims to warn all individual investors already invested in stocks and funds, and those who are seriously considering it, to be more diligent about and critical of investing in financial markets and those who want us to play their games. To achieve this goal, we will dive deeper into the mechanisms of investing—its structure, its main players, and the elements of gambling and chance. It is also necessary reading for a much wider range of specific and advanced topics, such as investment strategy, investment selection, or product categories such as mutual funds or exchange-traded funds.

Book Outline:

In the first part, we will take a look at pure investment theory, its history, and ramifications for society as a whole. In the second part, we will explore the commonalities between gambling and investing. We will observe investment banks and brokers, their financial incentives, and how they encourage players to play their games. It will also cover these same institutions—whom I call "game facilitators."

Finally, this book will examine how the odds are systematically stacked against the majority of players, through the frictional cost of fees, elaborate deceptions, and fraud within games and the entire financial system. On a more positive note, the book will demonstrate that individuals always have their edge that they can use. It will show that we all have a choice, and that there are valid alternatives to Wall Street games. Most importantly, I will introduce a simple strategy that anybody can follow when embarking on the treacherous seas of investing.

Because I am an independent investor and writer, (and to quote Matt Damon), "not running for any kind of office, I can say pretty much whatever I want,"[3] I can, and will, be frank with you. I will shed more light on the darker side of financial market investing and its key players, but I will also demonstrate that investing is all about individual choices, that depends on understanding some simple economic principles. With the knowledge contained here, you may achieve returns that far surpass conventional returns, free of Wall Street institutional control.

PART I

THE RATIONAL DECISION

CHAPTER 1

———◆———

STRANGER THAN FICTION

"The exquisite truth is to believe in something that maybe you know is a fiction, but you believe in it willingly."
—Roberto Benigni

Have you ever wondered about the nature of money? Its tendency to flow out rather than in? There are powerful forces at hand that dictate the flow of wealth. Investing is part of this invisible force that moves money in our economic system, and, in free markets, plays a significant role in how scarce resources are allocated most efficiently. Investing is all about cash flows—how we command, control, and grow them. The best investors in the world just sit down and let the money flow into their pockets without much effort. Many consider it a game. In the following chapters, we will take a look at investing's true nature and see that it is very different from gambling and taking just chances.

The Roots of Investing: The One-to-One Deal

The word *invest* derives from the Latin *vestis* which means "clothing," and indeed the history of investment goes back at least as far as the Roman Empire. Indeed one of Rome's richest men, Marcus Crassus, was a notably savvy and skilled investor—and did rather well for himself until the Parthians poured molten gold down his throat. Investing has been an integral part of the enormous success story we as a species have enjoyed over the last 400 years. It is a crucial part of modern capitalism, where mass consumption and professional investing have become pillars of ever-more growth and progress. But, let's go back a little, to understand the true meaning of investing and its impact on society in human civilization.

Historically, investing has always been an individual activity. People made money, saved a portion of it and invested it in activities such as trade and farming.

Before the emergence of the first public financial markets, money for large and risky projects (particularly wars) was either raised through taxes or privately negotiated transactions between two parties. Kingdoms borrowing from wealthy merchant or banking families were the norm. They were then able to loot the conquered regions and impose new trade monopolies, while the lenders enjoyed higher status, profit, and access to new lands. For the conquerors, glory, honor and a place in the history books or heaven also worked as an incentive to risk their lives and fortunes. The Athenians, for example, financed large warships to assert their commercial and political interest throughout Greece and the Mediterranean. A few individual Romans financed entire private armies through their trading activities and commercial interests.

Christopher Columbus negotiated a private contract with King Ferdinand and Queen Isabella, which stipulated his share of potential profits—plus fancy titles, such as *Admiral of the Ocean Sea* and *Viceroy and Governor* of the Indies. In return for financing the expedition, Ferdinand and Isabella would receive the majority of the profits and a place in heaven for spreading the Christian faith. Put another way; the Spanish crown got access to future returns from any land discovered, and Columbus got money to *finance* a whole fleet and his expedition. Needless to say, the Native- American tribes were not consulted on how they felt about all this.

One-to-one deals are, hence, the bedrock of human investing activity, but there are some serious drawbacks. At times, the negotiating process in private transactions can get messy, as both parties want to make sure that all their rights and duties are clearly stated, and no misunderstandings occur along the way. All negotiated deals tend to have structural weaknesses and loopholes; and when deals go sour, they must be solved in front of local authorities, which means involving another party.

Liquidity is another issue. After Queen Isabella of Spain finally opened her purse to Columbus, it took several years to see her money returned. Indeed, the first slaves and gold nuggets Columbus brought back from his first expedition were, from her point of view, pretty disappointing. It wasn't until her descendants' time that Spain had the infrastructure to capitalize on the New

World's vast silver deposits, and to create huge tobacco and sugar plantations on the backs of millions of laboring slaves.

The Emergence of Stock Markets

Unfortunately for the Spanish, despite being catapulted into the position of a global superpower, their wealth and power did not last. Many of their European holdings rebelled against Spanish supremacy and wanted their independent share of the riches that lay overseas. One such nation was the small area of today's modern Netherlands, and its commercial center, Amsterdam.

By the 16th-century, everyone in Europe knew of the enormous potential riches that an organized and well-financed overseas expedition could achieve. In the century or so after Columbus' "discovery," several Dutch vessels returning from Southeast Asia had returned with cargoes full of spices, gold, and precious stones. What was needed was a reliable system that would provide a consistent stream of money to finance such missions, whatever the size- a system that would incentivize people to give freely and voluntarily. Raising capital from several investors in smaller amounts had its advantages, rather than being dependent on kingdom's coffers, or the few leading banking and merchant families of Europe. Most important, though, was that it was a system that guaranteed that any money loaned or invested would be returned in full and with a fair share of profits. A system like that had the benefit of opening up the field for stock investing to the public, meaning that the risk of the venture is spread over thousands of small commitments, and not one or two major financial packages from one or two major sponsors.

The Dutch created an innovation that allowed such a system to emerge—the joint stock company. The most famous was called the *Vereenigde Oostindische Compagnie* (VOC), known in English as the Dutch East India Company. For many scholars, the VOC's founding in 1602 was one of the most important events in the history of modern capitalism. With their publicly secured liquidity, the VOC established a trade route on a longer, but quicker route over the sea to the 'East Indies'—the area today known as Indonesia. It financed military operations against less cooperative natives and other competing colonial powers such as Spain.

Control of the company was held tightly by its directors; ordinary shareholders did not have much influence on the company's direction or access to accounting statements—this was long before management had come to live for "shareholder value." The company paid generous dividends, and hence a lot of other players wanted in. As intended, they gave their money freely.

One of the stipulations of this so-called *aktie*, the Dutch word for stock, was that the money invested was non-refundable. However, there were always cases where investors wanted out, due to financial emergencies or cold feet. And so, the first stock exchange in Amsterdam emerged; sellers could exchange their shares for cash from willing buyers. People could bid on the few shares that were available for purchase, and sellers could demand more than they'd initially paid on the basis of the stock's likelihood of providing a safe return. The economic law of supply and demand could determine the market price at any day of trading, and the exchange would stand in between buyer and sellers as a neutral party.

The Dutch East India company and many similar enterprises that followed had a voracious appetite for more capital to fund their ever-expanding operations overseas. As long as the ships returned full of riches, investors were assured, and the value of their individual stocks continued to rise and raise the prices higher. But no market is stable forever.

The Definition of Investing

In purely financial terms, investing is often described as "the process of laying out money now, in the expectation of receiving more money in the future." And,- "the act of committing money or capital to an endeavor (a business, project, real estate, etc.) with the expectation of obtaining an additional income or profit."[4]

There is an alternative definition to the above that I prefer and would like you to consider. It comes from Benjamin Graham, the intellectual father of modern value investing and financial analysis:

"An investment operation is one which, upon thorough analysis, promises safety of principal and an adequate return. Operations not meeting these requirements are speculative."[5]

According to this definition, there are two components to investing: capital protection and adequate returns. Let's have a closer look at each core component of his definition and their relationship to each other in the following chapters.

CHAPTER 2

———•◆•———

CAPITAL AND PROPERTY

"Capital is money, capital is commodities. By virtue of it being value, it has acquired the occult ability to add value to itself. It brings forth living offspring, or, at the least, lays golden eggs."
— Karl Marx

Investing your capital, besides its financial incentives, allows for the efficient distribution of access to money to where it is needed most. Hence, investing is important for world organizations, single states, communities, and individuals. You, as an individual, play a major role in this economic structure. Your investments are an economic resource that can create jobs, develop new technologies and help accelerate the development of human life and society as a whole. Your investments, if made properly, will enable you to see your wealth increase through either annual returns or modest capital increases. It provides each individual with more capital that can be reinvested in new investment projects, which repeats the cycle of growth and prosperity.

Investors needed some objective references and structure for deciding to where to put their precious capital, leading to the development valuing property on the basis of understanding risk and return. In this chapter, we will have a look at capital protection through the rights of property ownership and the mechanism of assessing the fair value of any investment to further reduce risk.

Personal property

In early civilization and throughout history, merchants and farmers made independent investment decisions based on the data they had available, without being able to predict the future or even the understanding of the basics of economic activity. Additionally, they constantly had to deal with the uncertainty of having their capital returned. The fiction of universal trust in credit and a better financial future still did not exist at that time. So even before people could engage in any sort of investing at all, there needed to be a consensus on what, exactly, was being invested in. In other words, people needed a generalized concept of *private property*, before they could even begin to consider taking their property and increasing its value.

Without the notion of *property*—more specifically, the *right to own property*—we'd still be fighting like barbarians, killing and ravaging villages, states, and other countries, just to get other people's possessions and wealth. Hence, private property is one of the first things covered in early law codes. Eventually, and as early as the reign of Hammurabi in Babylonia (c. 1810-1750 BC), there were clear concepts of a debtor and debt – that is, the idea that *someone owns something exclusively*, but can *temporarily give possession* (but not ultimate ownership) to someone else. Crucially, this was all done with the understanding that *they would have to give it back at an agreed time*.

Over time, these contracts have become more elaborate and complicated, with each one having their set of unique stipulations and terms. Today, if you hear people talk about investing in real estate, stocks or bonds, they are basically referring to different types of sophisticated contracts that protect their property. The bottom line is this: *the laws and conventions which handle the movement of wealth are the most important part of any financial system*. As we shall see, it is through manipulating and controlling these codes that the world's elites maintain and justify maintaining their wealth.

Having your property protected by law does not mean that you are protected from entering financially unfavorable contracts that would result in a loss of money. What is paid for an asset and what is gotten in return, is entirely the investor's responsibility. Therefore, one of an investor's primary responsibilities is ascertaining what kind of contract is being entered into, and having, at the very minimum, an understanding of the underlying asset. As a good friend and professional investor once told me about adding something to my investment portfolio, "You should date a bit before you make a final decision."

Another essential framework is *valuation* and *valuation theory*. Valuation, determining the value of an investment, has become the single most important factor in making more informed investment decisions.

Unfortunately, valuing an economic asset has also been the starting point for some amount of skullduggery and corruption. How do we value something today on the basis of uncertain returns in the future? What are the odds of money flowing back into our pockets, and more importantly, how much? And how much money would be in it for you? Take Google Inc. for example (now Alphabet Inc.). We all know the company, we all use it, and we all know they made $16.3 billion in 2015 and most likely have a bright future ahead. But how do you value the company, exactly, without accessing all sorts of data you don't have? More specifically, what price should be paid today to receive the value we hope to receive? Whereas this relationship is apparent when purchasing consumer goods, it is much more complicated for investments, and learning to handle the difference is crucial to success.

Baseline Valuation

If you buy something for your home (i.e., a piece of furniture), this new item is your property; and in accounting terms, it will be booked in your asset column of your personal balance sheet. The left-hand column lists all your possessions, usually in order of liquidity, i.e. how quickly we could turn it into cash. You start with cash, gold, and all your jewelry first and end with your house, your cars, everything you've ever bought.

Now, this left-hand column has a tendency to decline over time, if you don't add anything new. One reason is that most consumer items decay over time. But if you had just to sell everything you own, you could do so at an estate auction, when entire households are auctioned off. The money you would get through liquidating your entire asset column at short notice is an investor's *base valuation model*. Professionals call it the *liquidation value*.

Imagine, though, if we sold all of Google's physical assets today—all the crazy and colorful furniture, massive servers and candy bars from their offices around the world, we wouldn't get much. At least, nothing close to Google's listed *market capitalization* of more than $500 billion in the middle of 2016. So where does that figure come from? What constitutes and explains this massive discrepancy between liquidation valuation?

Cash Flows

The difference can be easily explained by the money that flows into Google's pockets on a daily basis. This is known as cash inflow or *free cash flow*. Free cash flow just means the money in your pockets, the net of all monthly financial obligations and money spent to maintain existing operations. It is these cash flows today, and into the future, that makes Google so valuable.

If you ever wanted to put a price tag on yourself, you would use the same rationale. If you add all cash you would ever earn over a lifetime, and add all our possessions at liquidation prices at the end of your life, discounted by the risk-free rate that represents our opportunity cost (more on this topic later), you could, roughly estimate your personal value today.

In reality, this is certainly much more complex. As an individual, the capacity to earn money in the future grows over the lifetime of a career, and the risk-free rate might change dramatically, as it has so many times before. Your personal value increases with your earnings potential, i.e. the potential to increase your salary over time. Unfortunately, we all have only a vague idea of our future earnings potential, so your personal price tag varies, depending on the investments in yourself or your personal achievement at your current job. The more relevant data we have available, the easier it is to assess one's monetary value. The price tag of a commercial banker with ten years of experience is much easier to calculate than a teenager's value. The teen may grow up to be the lead singer of the world's most successful rock band — but then again, may not. The commercial banker, on the other hand, is probably going to make $200k next year plus a considerable bonus. Given a choice, who would you invest in?

The Chicken Conundrum

To demonstrate the power of cash flows, and the effects it has on the price of investment opportunities, I would like to introduce my friend, the Cash Flow Valuation Chicken.

Let's assume you have a chicken that lays an egg every day, an egg which you sell to your neighbor for $1. After a month, you have sold 30 eggs, so you have $30 in your pocket (minus all the chicken feed for a month).

Now imagine your neighbor wants to borrow that chicken for a month. How much would you charge your neighbor for that rental period? It makes sense to charge him $30, right? That's what your chicken would be worth if you kept it for yourself.

But let's imagine that, the day before your mother's birthday, you neighbor comes to you and says he'll pay you $27 for your $30 chicken. You don't want to say yes, of course, because it's $3 less than you would have made. But, you know, and your neighbor knows, that there is no other way you have of securing money before your mother bursts into tears because, yet again, you forgot she was turning 43. So you take the $27 and call it a day—because 90% of the price is surely better than 0%, right?

Now, it turns out your neighbor is the crafty sort. He's sold all those eggs to *his* wealthy friend, who has plenty of money, for $1.50 each, and made $45 already! So, from your neighbor's perspective, he has $42 minimum (subtracting about $3 for feed, etc.), minus $27 rental, earning him a nice profit of $15.

Your neighbor was able to do so because he had a pure information advantage – namely, that his wealthy friend would be happy to buy an egg for 50% more than he would. Among investors, we call this a *mispriced investment*—one that was undervalued due to the missing information.

But then, disaster! The rich customer finds out about the price markup and now will only pay $1 per egg like everyone else. So the next year, your neighbor won't rent the chicken for $27. He does remember, though, that your mother's birthday is soon. He's a good man and wants to help you out, so he offers to rent it for $15. Less than last year; but since you need the money now, you take the deal. This time, he sold 28 eggs and made the expected $28 in revenues minus the $15 rental price—a nice net profit of $13. Again, not a bad return on investment. And again, he had a simple information advantage: he knew that your mother's birthday was coming, she always wants expensive presents, and you're always broke this time of year. Again, the bet or investment was mispriced from his point of view, with almost no risk for him.

Returning to investing, any investment *needs to be valued on the basis of its future cash flows* to determine a price you would be willing to pay *today*. This is where even the most intelligent, experienced, and most informed market participants make mistakes. They overpay, make ridiculous assumptions, and later sell in panic when cold reality sets in. Why do investors make errors in such predictable fashion? Why do they continually overpay for something even though they are aware their assumptions might be a bit on the optimistic side? There are three logical explanations for this:

1. They have no intention of investing in the proper sense of the word. They just want to speculate on rising prices. For example, speculating that egg prices will increase dramatically, or the demand for chickens suddenly increase. The chicken itself is not important.
2. They overpay for investment by miscalculating future cash flows. Humans tend to be overly optimistic, especially in a conducive environment. Hoping that a chicken would lay two eggs a day instead of one, because that is what everybody else believes and is promoted by chicken salespeople.
3. They just didn't know what they were buying in the first place. They thought they bought a wool-giving sheep, but received an egg-laying chicken.

What we can take away from this: know your chicken, and don't overpay for it.

Financial Markets

In the above chicken example, both parties negotiated a private contract and all its terms between the lender and borrower. This is often time-consuming and inefficient. This is why financial markets are so important for our economic system today. They don't only raise capital for people with ideas and expansion plans, but they also put a price on vast amounts of financial assets around the world, ranging from equities to bonds and complex financial products. By so doing, they provide all players with a daily reminder of their wealth.

Delving deeper, the functions of financial markets can be divided into *raising capital for businesses* on one hand, and providing a place where buyers and sellers of issued securities *agree on prices* on the other. This latter function is much more potent in creating and destroying fortunes. Among professionals, these two functions are known as primary and secondary markets, and we will learn more about them below.

Primary markets are where actual money is raised for the party that needs capital. The most common image a bystander might have of primary markets is that of stock exchanges, such as in New York, London or Tokyo, and their regular IPOs (Initial Public Offering). When a private company goes public and sells its shares to the public, it can either raise capital by issuing new shares or simply sell its existing shares from early investors. An IPO also gives permanent access to public companies, in order to raise more capital, if the need arises.

Today, as in the past, shares can only be sold and transformed back into cash by selling to other investors, usually through an agent or a broker—*"game facilitators."*

The secondary market's purpose has nothing to do with raising money, as no money flows to the corporation which issued these securities in the first place. For instance, when you buy shares of Google through an online broker, no money flows to Google. Someone who previously owned the same shares of Google decided to sell. In this world, Google might not even exist. It could be an imaginary entity. The question would then be at what price should one investor sell to the next investor. That is where secondary markets reveal their real power and influence over investors.

The Pricing of Everything

A theory states that asset prices fully reflect all available information, and hence financial products such as stocks *always trade at their fair value*; over- or undervaluation can therefore never exist. This is somehow contradictory to another common law of economics—the law of supply and demand. Basic economic theory of supply and demand teaches us that price quotations are a function of the *immediate* demand and supply for the item in question. When there is high demand for goods or services, but the supply is limited, the price automatically goes up, regardless of the long-term outlook. We can observe this phenomenon when we go on vacation and have to deal with in-season prices. The same idea applies when we buy luxury brand items. A handbag that has a highly sought after brand name can be ten times more valuable in the eye of the beholder than the same bag produced in the same factory without this particular brand logo. So how can we always have fair prices, when there is an unreasonable or even irrational demand for goods or services? It gets fascinating when we add the element of deception and supply and demand manipulation to the price equation.

The real issue is that future cash flows for most private business investments and even real estate investments vary and fluctuate. It can drop or rise depending on the economic environment, or even seasons. For new business ventures operating in the field of High-Tech, pharmacy, and biotechnology, we don't have a conclusive set of data that would allow us to make any constructive estimates about cash flows far into the unknown future. We are like the early explorers searching for new riches in far distant regions, but risking our wealth (but not our lives). It is this hope and imagination of future wealth that keeps any financial expedition alive.

For investors, today's known cash flows are stories of the past, and what really counts are future imagined cash flows. Here is where the fiction starts. In our Google example, if the majority of Google's shareholders believe that the company can grow its future cash flows substantially, higher market prices are justifiable today. Unfortunately, nobody knows if any particular scenario comes to fruition. There is the factor of uncertainty; the unknown that makes things so interesting for investors and punters alike.

However, uncertainty is only a function of how much you don't know. In other words, the more you know, the less uncertain you are about your investment. It is only natural to assume that business insiders might be better equipped to anticipate future growth and revenue streams of their operations in question. Outsiders, by definition, have less insight, unless they have access to management or do detailed research and investigative work. The broad masses (i.e., you and me) will be at the very bottom of the information food chain, as we have no clue about what actually goes on internally. More investors than you think just formulate views based on other people's opinion and captivating promotional campaigns, in the hope the bet will pay out in the future. They take risks; they take chances.

CHAPTER 3

───────◆───────

RETURNS AND CHANCE

"Take calculated risks. That is quite different from being rash."—George S. Patton Jr.

What are adequate returns and why are they so important? Adequate returns compensate investors for handing over their scarce resource—money. Investors want money, and they want more money, in real terms, after inflation and any tax obligations. But what is *adequate*? 1%, with a capital guarantee (Even though 100% guarantees have never existed in the world of investing)? Or should we consider 15%? Why not 25, or even 50% per annum? Before the idea of stock markets and capital markets, money lenders were only willing to give up their money in small amounts, short-term, and at high-interest rates. Today, if you borrow money from more dubious sources connected to the underworld, the same principles apply. Anybody making a decision to pass money, from their pocket's to someone else's, have to understand two things – money, and risk.

Money and Investing

One of the catalysts for humans founding cities and empires "was probably the appearance of fiction," notes Yuval Harari, author of *Sapiens*. "Large numbers of strangers can cooperate successfully by believing in common myths. Any large-scale human cooperation – whether a modern state, a medieval church, an ancient city or an archaic tribe – is rooted in common myths that exist only in people's collective imagination."[6]

Think about that—*money* is not "real." Money is a purely intellectual notion, a complex one, whose rules are entirely derived from one set of relationships: trust and uncertainty among participants in the market. What humans have created complex, imaginative systems that build on each other out of pure nothingness. Investing is one such imaginary system. It is a fiction that is based on the concept of money, a very complex topic in its own right.

Money is just a medium for exchanging goods and services, but it also functions as a storage of wealth. It requires trust and faith that the future will be as good or better than the present, and hence the money you're handing over—a promise on a piece of paper to give whoever holds it '100 dollars' or whatever—will still have value in the future. Money in this process undergoes a magical transformation from the humble $100 you have in your hand to all those wonderful things you imagine buying. With a savvy investment, that money may turn into yachts, gold watches, and trips to Aruba.

However, what we receive and what we pay are two very different concepts. As we have seen, it favors the party who has an information advantage. Demanding adequate returns are one way to compensate investors for the risks of passing their money to another party. The higher they perceive the risks involved, the higher the returns they need to demand. However, this is just a general guideline and prone to misunderstandings and confusion.

Let's consider the safest form of investing today—short-term U.S. government notes and bonds of up to 10 years or more. Investors can be assured that they first get their invested principal returned in full, and on top of that, will receive a pre-agreed semi-annual or annual interest payment. These cash flows are guaranteed by the U.S. government and backed by U.S. taxpaying citizens, as well as a vast military arsenal that sees U.S. political and economic interests enforced throughout the world. Investments very similar to U.S. Treasury bonds are bonds issued by the German and Japanese government called *Bunds* and *JGBs* (Japanese Government Bonds). Both countries are ranked among the safest investments in the world and are considered "safe havens" for your money, even though they yield even less than U.S. Treasury bonds in 2016.

Nevertheless, the U.S. Treasury's yield is the benchmark return, or risk-free rate, for all other investments in the world to compare itself with. It represents the opportunity cost of all other possible investments. It's a core principle in finance known as the "time value of money." What time value means is cash in your hand is much more valuable than the same amount of cash in an uncertain future. It is understood in the industry that every other competing investment that is considered less safe should pay an appropriate premium over this opportunity cost in order to make it more attractive for investors to open their wallets. Otherwise, we would just buy safe U.S. Treasury bonds for the same returns. But here is the problem. What would be an appropriate premium over risk-free rate? How much more should investors demand, if the risk-free-rate is zero or even negative? Clearly, it must be connected to how we perceive risk in each other investments than safe government bonds. An early start-up investment should require a much higher risk premium than a corporate bond issued by General Electric. But how do you quantify the difference? This is where most investors and academic researchers differ in opinion, ranging from what actually constitutes investment risk and how to measure it. More importantly, how much exactly investors should demand for the additional risk they take on.

The Matter of Risk

So, what exactly is risk? The word "risk" derives from the Early Italian word *risicare*, which means "to dare." In investment, risk is the probability that you lose part, or all, of your investment. Whenever you lay out money, you will expose yourself to the risk of not getting the money you initially paid back. It is the same whether you buy stocks, bonds, real estate, or part interest in a private business. There are many different types of risks investors should be aware of and have to deal with, from the academic view theoretical risk to the risk of fraud we could experience on any level of the investment process. But to better understand risk, we need to look at the main reasons how and why investors lose money. For that, we need to look at the types of risk an individual investor has to deal with.

Overpayment Risk

By far the most relevant risk investors face is *overpayment risk*. This is the risk that paying too much for an asset can lead to financial losses. Let me give you a fairly recent example: Anthony Bolton, former star fund manager at Fidelity, came out of retirement to manage the *Chinese Special Situations Fund* for Fidelity between 2009 and 2014. He was so excited about the future prospect of China and its upcoming economic boom that he couldn't resist putting his financial magic on one of Fidelity's leading funds one last time. In hindsight, he might have wished to stay in retirement.

The first two years of the fund saw him performing well. Global stock markets quickly recovered from market lows in 2009, and he felt assured that he still had what it takes to be a leading fund manager. Then, during the disastrous year of 2011, he saw all of his gains melt away with a staggering loss of 34% for the year.

What happened? What had gone so wrong so quickly? One major contributing factor was a 90% loss of a single investment in China Integrated Energy, a company that claimed to be a producer of ethanol. The company was recommended to him by one of his previous investments, a United States-listed fund called Vision Opportunities. Bolton met with CIE's senior management, a standard procedure for all professional investors, to get a better picture of their business. Impressed by what he had seen, Bolton bought shares and built up a sizeable position for his China fund. "They told a good story," he later said.

Unfortunately, he didn't know as much about the company as he should have. At the same time Bolton was putting his money into CIE, someone else had hired investigators who went to one of the company's plants and stuck a camera outside. What they found astonished everyone. In Bolton's own words:

"...nothing was going on [at the factory]. But the next day, when another investor tour turned up, everything ramped up and started working again. A day later everything stopped again."[7]

In the end, investors realized the company did not have any operations at all. It was pure fiction and fantasy. They bought an empty shell company and lost a lot of money in the process. Bolton cut his losses and bailed on the investment, then canceled his investment with Vision Opportunities Fund for good measure. Bolton's experience is a simple example of overpayment risk. He didn't get nearly the value he was hoping for. You could argue that Bolton was a victim of fraud. Very often, overpaying for something is connected to a form of deception or even fraud. The point is that Bolton should have known more about the company he was investing in. Caveat emptor still applies to star fund managers.

Let's take a look at an example from our daily lives. When you go shopping, you could end up with low-quality goods; they could be damaged, fake, or not as nice as you'd thought they'd be. What follows is an instant realization that you *overpaid* for something. Unfortunately, buyer's remorse is a little different when it involves financial assets for two reasons. First, the real value of a stock is more difficult to assess than that of an object like a bottle of Coca Cola. Second, the true value of the stock only becomes apparent to the investor long after it's been purchased. A bad steak is obvious, but a rotten stock can take months to stink. More upsetting, perhaps, is the fact that there are only two things that cause such purchases to go ahead:

1. Wishful thinking.
2. Insufficient knowledge.

Naïve tourists buying souvenirs and antiques in a foreign country get regularly scammed for those two reasons. *If you don't know what you're purchasing, you are just taking an unnecessary risk.*

Force Majeure

The second type of risk is called *force majeure*. To explain this, I am going to tell you the story of a farmer. Takahashi Saito (not his real name) is a farmer in Sendai, Miyagi Prefecture in the northeastern region of Japan. In early 2011, when he bought some fertile land from a retiring farmer he'd known for decades, Saito was convinced he had gotten a great piece of land at a fair price. The owner chipped in some farming equipment and a bunch of puppies, happy to see that his land was being managed by a younger, capable farmer who would carry on the local traditions. He signed the papers, local rice wine flowed and toasts were given. It was the beginning of a close relationship between him and his new community. Or so he thought.

Little did Takahashi know that his entire investment would literally sink into the abyss on the afternoon of March 11, 2011. In the aftermath of the biggest recorded earthquake in Japanese history, Saito's new land was ravaged by tsunamis laden with mud and industrial waste. Any hope Saito may have had of recovering his investment disappeared over the next few days as the Fukushima nuclear disaster unfolded. By the end of the week, his land was off-limits entirely, as it lay within the 40 km (25 miles) exclusion zone around the power station.

All investors in history have had to face the aspect of major unforeseen events such as natural catastrophes or wars. All those random events and unexplainable incidents outside of their control or influence. Events that Nassim Taleb titled as "Black

Swan" event, "that comes as a surprise, has a major effect, and is often inappropriately rationalized after the fact with the benefit of hindsight."[8] This is something any investor has to live with: the risk of uncertainty and the aspect of chance in our lives. By their very nature, these incidents are hard to predict, which is why in the world, they're known as acts of God. There are only two ways to account for the acts of God – constant vigilance and diversifying investments to ensure that the disaster doesn't destroy all of them.

Risk of Financial Leverage

There are many additional types of risks in investment, but one category of risk that caused so much havoc in the world of finance and investing is the risk of financial leverage. This risk of loss increases exponentially when we add any form of "financial leverage," which is just a fancy way of saying "borrowing money to play." If you use any financial leverage, you magnify not only your potential gains but also your potential losses. When investors use excessive financial leverage, the risk of loss increases dramatically, even if mathematical models tell you otherwise. The money borrowed still has to be paid back within an agreed period, and usually ends up with less favorable interest rates.

Also, with borrowed money, investors expose themselves to the potential of being forced out of positions, as lenders usually demand collateral for outstanding loans in challenging market environments. This can sometimes result in the need to close promising investment positions at a loss in order to provide the necessary liquidity. This usually happens at the most inconvenient time for investors, and results in a vicious cycle of falling prices and even more pressure to come up with new collateral. Though leverage might enhance performance dramatically, it also makes investment decisions much more complicated.

Good Financial Leverage

Leverage can be the rocket fuel to enormous riches, *as long as none of your own money is involved*. In the financial world, this is referred to as "good leverage." It is when you buy investments entirely with other people's money and get a cut of the winnings. If you win, you get a percentage cut of the gains; if you lose, your pride might get hurt, but in the end, it wasn't your own money that was lost.

Investment banks and professional asset managers use this model with gusto, and they have made fortunes for themselves. Today, some funds still charge 2% management fees up front and 20% performance fees off of all profits. You're lending them money, and you actually pay them for this privilege. I call it a business model made in heaven.

Moronic Leverage

You borrow the maximum amount of money possible with your private wealth as collateral and take excessive risks. The wager either doesn't work, or you underestimate and miscalculate the real risks involved, and you lose it all, including your own wealth. That might seem to be a far-fetched scenario, but let's look at a real life case of this actually happening: Long-Term Capital Management (LTCM).

LTCM is the leading investment fund (a.k.a. a hedge fund) that blew up in the midst of the Russian financial crisis in 1998. It pushed the entire U.S. financial system to the brink of disaster way before Lehman Brothers finally succeeded ten years later. At times, it was leveraged 28:1 and more, i.e. *for every dollar they possessed*, they had borrowed $28. So although LTCM had around $1 billion in assets, they were able to buy over $28 billion worth of investments. It was rumored that LTCM had at its peak over $125 billion in assets with a capital base of only $4.7 billion.[9] Considering they mostly traded with other people's money, many partners decided to put all of their private wealth on the line as personal collateral to maximize their personal profit potential. LTCM was on the quest to find that perfect investment formula that promised endless riches and easy gains on the assumption that risk can be measured as easily as gravity. The top management at LTCM truly believed that they had found the perfect formula, as shown in their overconfidence in betting *their own fortunes* in their company.

LTCM simply ignored the fact that markets occasionally behave irrationally. When participants lose faith in academic models and assumptions that build the basis for these formulas and models, fiction deflates to nothingness and only facts and reality are the foundation for a hard landing. When players sell in panic and fear takes hold of markets, no rationally-explained formula or story of a better future will be able to stop the financial onslaught of ever falling prices and increasing losses. LTCM underestimated their greed and were overconfident in their ability to consistently anticipate the future correctly.

To this day, when interviewed, LTCM's key partners believed that their risk was practically zero in accordance with their financial models. They still believe that they would have made money on their bets had they survived. Their argument is that LTCM was just overwhelmed by the irrationality of markets that their mathematical models just couldn't account for. Their lenders and investors who'd lost billions in the blow-up and the central bankers who'd done the utmost to avoid a collapse of the entire financial system couldn't disagree more, regardless of irrational market players and unexpected events. In the wake of LTCM's collapse, many partners literally lost it all—luxurious mansions, yachts, cars, and status.

Key Takeaways

In this part, we learned the background and origins of investing. Its nature and elementary components. We have looked at ways to assure the return of capital through contracts protected by law. But a contract itself doesn't protect an investor from possible losses. In order to assure "safety of principle," as Benjamin Graham postulates, you need to have a mechanism to evaluate and value each investment before a decision is made. We learned that in each case in order to protect our capital investment, we always have to make sure to understand the underlying asset we purchase and the rights we receive as property owners. Only then can we assess whether an investment promises *safety of principal*.

With Graham's second component of his investment definition, we looked at returns, as adequate compensation for the risks we take. Risk is understood as per definition, the possibility of losing real money. Furthermore, we looked at the importance of the risk-free rate as the reference point to compare all investment opportunities in a possible investment universe. We saw that the ultimate risk investors face is the risk of overpayment relative to the value they have hoped to receive, whether in real assets or future cash flows. We can say that investors need to take risk in order to achieve returns, but to minimize the real risk of loss, its potential to generate future cash flow needs to be assessed relative to the price paid. In Part II we transition from the topic of investing to the more glittery and exhilarating world of gambling and speculation.

PART II

THE METAMORPHOSIS

CHAPTER 4

---◆---

GAMBLING, INVESTING, AND SPECULATION

"All the evidence shows that God was actually quite a gambler, and the universe is a great casino, where dice are thrown, and roulette wheels spin on every occasion."
—Stephen Hawking

Risk has always been a part of human life. For early hominids, coming down from the trees and walking across the wide African plains was a huge risk to take, considering the sheer number of much more powerful predators in the open savannah who were waiting for an easy lunch. Gambles have changed the course of history, and Adam Smith, the author of the *Wealth of Nations*, acknowledged that the tendency for humans to take wagers here and there could foster even more economic progress. However, in excess, it can be catastrophic. Two centuries after Smith, John Maynard Keynes noted, "When the capital development of a country becomes the byproduct of the activities of a casino, the job is likely ill-done."[10] But he also believed that "[i]f human nature felt no temptation to take a chance...there might not be much investment merely as a result of cold calculation."

You could say that our capitalistic system relies on the "propensity of all its participants to take gambles in order to propel economic progress." If humans have no incentives to risk capital, scientific and technological progress, economic growth might be seriously hampered. But not even Smith and Keynes could have been 100% correct all the time on the issue of when to take a wager and, more importantly, when to stop. So how is one supposed to know?

A lot of what you read or hear about investing and financial markets is gambling. But that is not to say that the two are identical, or work the same way in practice. In today's markets, you'll, by and large, see two kinds of people: the speculator and the investor. The former is much closer to being a gambler than the latter; their approach is fundamentally that of a professional gambler. These days, many players in financial markets that are considered "investors" are in fact, speculators.

In this chapter, we'll see how most speculators use the same strategies and thinking in their investing as gamblers, and how real investors play a different game altogether.

The Money Game and Wall Street

Before we go deeper, let's define what I mean by "The Money Game" and "Wall Street," two terms that have captivated generations of players and seekers of fortune.

The money game is the entire process of investing within the current system. I don't call it simply "investing," because, as we'll see, it's more akin to the structural model of casinos where huge institutions facilitate people's entry into the process in order to profit off them. Hence, success and failure become a competition between the investor and institutions—*the money game*.

According to the late George J. W. Goodman, author of *The Money Game* (1976); it *"is about image and reality and identity and anxiety and money...The money which can preoccupy so much of our consciousness is an abstraction and a symbol. The game we create with it is an irrational one, and we play it better when we realize that, even as we try to bring rationality to it."*[11]

The most powerful and captivating games for money can be found on Wall Street. Whether we talk about stocks, mutual funds or exotic financial products, we truly have games on our hands with no equal. These games promise us an endless stream of entertainment and, more importantly, a possibility of riches that has only existed in our wildest imaginations.

Wall Street, however, has made this a reality for a few. Today, it's much more than just a single street in New York. It is, in fact, the collective name "for the financial and investment community, which includes all exchanges and large banks, brokerages, securities and underwriting firms, and big businesses."[12] Foremost, it symbolizes the brokerage, investment banking, and money management firms that sponsor, control, and dominate the money game.

The Gambler

Theoretically, investing and gambling are very different ideas. That does not mean that they don't share some common traits, and it is precisely the failure of people to understand how investing should be different than gambling that creates so many problems. To explain the crucial difference between the two, we first need to understand precisely what gambling is.

Gambling, according to the standard definition, "is the wagering of money or something of value (often referred to as "the stakes") on an event with an uncertain outcome with the primary intent of winning additional money and/or material goods."[13] Peter L. Bernstein, the author of *Against the Gods*, has called it "the very essence of risk taking."[14]

According to this definition, any decision involving making money that involves pure uncertainty are gambles because they incur the possibility of financial loss. On the other hand, gambling also promises untold riches. It is precisely this fascination for creating riches out of nothingness that has captivated and ruined generations of gamblers.

William Poundstone, in his book *Fortune's Formula*, had a great example: "In 2004, a London man named Ashley Revell sold all his possessions, including his clothes, and staked his entire net worth of $135,300 on a roulette wheel at the Plaza Hotel in Las Vegas. Revell wore a rented tuxedo and bet on red. He won. He decided against going for double or nothing." It was a good decision. In American Roulette, the chance of him winning again on either color is 46.37%. You might ask yourself why only 46.37, and not fifty. Well, you might have noticed the green zeros on the wheel. This is called a house edge: the advantage the casino holds over the player. In American roulette, the house edge is about 5.60%.

According to Poundstone, "Revell was playing an unfavorable game. His actions would hardly have been less reckless had he had an edge. The *bet-it-all* policy works only until you lose." And that's the thing with gambling—it's all great until it isn't, and when it isn't, it is often catastrophically bad.

You see, all gamblers share one aspect of taking chances, known as the *gambler's ruin*. The original meaning is that "a gambler who raises his bet to a fixed fraction of bankroll when he wins, but does not reduce it when he loses, will eventually go broke, even if he has a positive expected value on each bet."[1515] Or, as Poundstone observed, "You can be the world's greatest poker player, backgammon player, or handicapper, but if you can't manage your bankroll, you'll end up broke. The sad fact is, almost everyone who gambles goes broke in the long run." In the first example above, we can intuitively understand this conundrum. If Ashley had continued to gamble in the same fashion, he would have eventually lost it all. Surprisingly or unsurprisingly, this doesn't deter many from trying to find riches in gambling. In taking chances on uncertain outcomes whatever the mathematical probability of win or loss are, you are bound to lose a few bets. Those who have very bad money management, i.e. bet more than they can afford to lose, will go broke. It is a mathematical certainty. As a dedicated investor, this might not directly apply to you, but it has indirect consequences for all of us when a few gamblers experience such a scenario. Keep that in mind for the rest of the book, as it will be mentioned later on.

The Speculator

According to Peter Bernstein, "Games of chance must be distinguished from games in which skill makes a difference."[16] Playing the lottery doesn't require any skills whatsoever. However, games such as poker or betting on horses can be influenced by the individual player's skill in determining possible outcomes. These are the games that depend on skill as well as luck. If you ever sat with a professional poker player to play a few rounds of poker, you would instantly understand the difference. Both of you might depend on luck to get good hands, but the professional poker would still beat you comfortably, due to his superior skills in anticipating and calculating the odds much faster and more accurately. A more mundane reason could be that your tells are just like an open book for anyone to exploit.

The professional gambler's close relative is the *speculator*. According to Benjamin Graham, a speculator's main aim is to make money quickly; "money in a hurry," as he puts it. Capital protection and the underlying yields, such as dividends or rental income, play only a limited role in decision-making. Speculators and professional gamblers alike make many decisions every day that directly influence their bankroll. A speculator's only way to win is to have an edge, by either being more accurate and quicker at calculating odds of each new game and allocating their money accordingly without going broke, or knowing something that the other players don't. If either applies, then they have an edge and the skills required to be professionals.

Graham himself was an avid speculator in his early days. He lost it all in one giant leveraged bet after the crash of 1929, and because he had borrowed a substantial amount of money, he was forced out of the markets for a longer period than he had wished.

Graham had an interesting take on speculators. He argued that those who are obsessed with minute price changes are only interested in changes they believe they can anticipate accurately with the help of their betting system. For example, if a central bank announces a new interest-rate policy on a set date, speculators anticipate price movement in currency markets and interest rate products sensitive to any such changes. They, then, place their bets before or immediately after such an event. Listed companies report their quarterly earnings and speculators aim to anticipate favorable price movements. The difference between the two actions could be a matter of a few seconds.

Hence, speculating involves a great deal of anticipating how many of the other players react to market news. On top of that, speculators almost always work with borrowed money to magnify their profits. These days, they trade in and out so many times that each small price change is meaningless unless it is magnified with borrowed money.

Today, the financial markets are dominated by speculators: professional and amateur. Ever-increasing trading volumes, daily volatility, and continuous increase in financial leverage has made it obvious that there are fortunes to be made, and they think they know how.

Speculating vs. Gambling

Let's take a look at the similarities and structural differences between gambling and speculating. How do they relate to each other and how can we distinguish between them?

If you compared betting on horse races or stock price movements, you could find many similarities. Betting on horses is as exciting, random, and unpredictable as betting on price movements. Like a giant board depicting the odds of various horses, the stock tickers also display information about falling and rising trends. But the information on both boards is useless, as they only depict the immediate past. At the tracks, you need to place your bets through bookies or at the race tracks. If you bet on price movements, you need to go through your online broker or private banker. In both cases, there are no 100% sure things, unless you rig the games, and even that has its risks. Like at the tracks, you are easily affected by how the majority of other bettors place their bets. In each case, seeing yourself alone on the other side of a bet or trade makes even the most experienced punter nervous.

There are, of course, many differences between a racetrack and a stock exchange. A horse must win, or at least place in a particular way, so there are only limited outcomes. For financial products and securities, such as stocks or funds, there is a whole sequence of possible outcomes. They can rise, fall, or have special events, such as dividend payments or mergers and hostile takeovers. Beyond that, each race has a predetermined ending, just like each bet at the roulette table or hand in a poker game. There is a reason, why *all-in games* in no-limit poker are so fascinating. This is in stark contrast to purchasing general financial products. A speculation could go on indefinitely. As long as the stock, real estate or fund exists, a player could decide to stay in the game, even if a short-term price speculation didn't pay off as expected.

But there is a more subtle difference between ordinary gamblers and speculators, and it lies in their attitudes on how they approach each bet. In a game where the outcome is determined by both chance and skill, the more skillful player wins in the long-term. Hence, one could argue that professional gamblers and speculators are just more skillful gamblers. As a matter of fact, no self-respecting speculator considers him or herself as an ordinary gambler; they tend to assume, on some level, that they are superior. Speculators feel that they are more capable of making rational, calculated bets. Their confidence is a result of the tools and technology they use. These days, they use powerful hardware, elaborate databases and complex software that can spit out hundreds of possible gambling scenarios in a millisecond.

Speculators and Risk

Speculators might be more skillful gamblers, but they still had to deal with an uncertain future when it came to anticipating price movements. They needed to calculate the odds of each bet with mathematical precision so that they could make more rational, and hence superior decisions than a common gambler. They needed to understand risk in a different way than traditional investors have been doing for centuries—more sophisticated and with more mathematical precision.

Academia was up to the task, and they based their theories on a relatively young mathematical concept derived from gambling—*probability theory* and *the laws of probability*. Three Frenchmen, (Chevalier de Méré, Blaise Pascal and Pierre de Fermat), are responsible for revolutionizing gambling and laying the groundwork for modern risk management. Chevalier de Méré, a notorious gambler, made history by challenging Blaise Pascal, a gifted mathematician, to explain his unexpected losses from gambling. In trying to solve this riddle Pascal turned to Pierre de Fermat, an equally gifted mathematician. In lengthy correspondences, they wrote each other about games of chance. Together they laid out the mathematical foundations for the theory of probability in 1654.

Over the following centuries, many more famous mathematicians contributed to the subject of probability. Jacob Bernoulli and Abraham de Moivre solidified the theory of probability within the academic field of mathematics, by showing how to calculate a wide range of complex probabilities. In 1713, Bernoulli proved a version of the fundamental law of large numbers, which states that "in a large number of trials, the average of the outcomes is likely to be very close to the expected value." For example, in 1,000 throws of a fair coin, it is likely that there are close to 500 heads. The larger the number of throws, the closer to half-and-half the proportion is likely to be.[17] Not much later, Thomas Bayes, a former English minister, offered the Bayes' theorem, which is another interpretation of the concept of probability. It demonstrates how to make better-informed decisions by mathematically blending new information with old information.

But, there was a challenge to convert the theories derived from gambling based on the simple acts of tossing a die or spinning the roulette wheel to the complex behavior of financial markets and its erratic price movement with a much wider range of outcomes. It needed to be based on numbers and lots of historical data to get any conclusive results about future price movements.

In 1917, Ladislaus Bortkiewicz achieved a breakthrough and added a missing piece to make modern risk management possible. Based on Bernoulli's work, he developed the field of *stochastic*: "A stochastic event or system is one that is unpredictable because of a random variable."[18] This is where the world of modern finance and academia got together. It finally provided a model for the study of random fluctuations in stock markets, leading to the use of sophisticated probability models in mathematical finance with *normal distributions* and *standard deviations*. It shaped the field of risk management as we know it, and it is used by insurance institutions and financial organizations around the world ever since.

For Wall Street, the concept of quantifying risk for financial markets was born. Central to much of this is the idea of the "*standard deviation.*" Standard deviation means the recorded volatility of a price instrument. A *high standard deviation* simply means *this investment is very risky*– it changes the price a lot. A stock that fluctuates 3% up and down on a daily basis is characterized as having a higher standard deviation than a stock that fluctuates 1% per day. In reverse, it also means that if you construct a portfolio where different holdings trade in exactly opposite directions based on historical data, the mathematical risk is assumed to be zero, as each financial instrument cancels its prices volatility. For example, if the price of investment A goes up, the price of investment B simultaneously goes down and for the same amount. This is what historical data has shown in the past. But here is the true magic—the theoretical volatility would be zero as the total investment of both would always be flat. Investors feel psychologically assured that everything is fine, all the while they collect income, such as dividends or interest payments. Now let's add some financial leverages, to the tune of 10:1 ratio and investors can make some serious money without worrying too much about risk. The portfolio risk is still zero, and they have just multiplied their income by ten. With a few simple tricks, we have created the finest financial alchemy.

This last part is crucial because it revolutionized professional investment management and finance. Speculators were able to create all sorts of new formulas, calculate all sorts of sophisticated investment portfolios, and all based on standard deviation and assumed a small risk. They finally made speculating "scientific," socially acceptable and imbued with a touch of real sophistication. Luckily, all the data necessary for these complex calculations was there and readily available. At the same time, the processing power to work with this data continuously increased from the early 1950s to cope with the new amount of data.

The numbers were magical, and it created a world where you could invest with an engineering precision, in a portfolio that had an overall calculated risk of zero. And you didn't have to be a financial genius to understand that. It is a sort of sleight-of-hand to convince people that there is *no risk* in handing over their money. Certainly, it is a grossly simplified explanation of how modern finance works today, but it explains the thought process of risk management departments around the world.

Here is where it went wrong. Right from the start, academics, scientists and financial punters lost all sense for the underlying assets upon which they based their theoretical construct. An overemphasis on market prices, as convenient data points for quantifying risk, have become the main focus ever since. The underlying asset of a stock price might as well be a *turd* wrapped in the finest silk and promoted on stock exchanges as having future growth potential—it would not matter, as long as speculators have their price data to base their risk calculations on.

The Investor

So far, we can say that each and every decision that involves placing money on an uncertain future to gain financial rewards is very much a gamble. That counts for investors as well. When formulating views on the future and placing money on these views, there is always a possibility of being wrong. It is how all parties approach these risks and aim to improve the odds that differentiate them, whether they are gamblers, speculators, or investors.

However, like in any game that is determined not only by the factor of chance but also the skills of their players, all parties aimed to improve their odds of winning by improving and honing their technical skills. All found their own elaborate ways to do so.

Gamblers swear by their betting system or superstition, while speculators calculate complex theories and models using tools like chart analysis and historical data analysis. Investors also rely on a vast amount of historical financial data, such as financial statements or industry reports. All this effort has one purpose: improving their odds of experiencing a positive outcome. Unsurprisingly, everyone has great faith and trust in their respective systems. However, there is an obvious difference.

Where gamblers or speculators care only about the immediate bet and its dualistic outcome of winning or losing, investors are concerned about the underlying asset. Rather than anticipating absolute price changes in a binary manner, investors make use of the fact that betting on financial assets offer a wider range of possible outcomes. Prices could go sideways, but the asset itself throws off monthly rental income, semi-annual dividends or interests. Prices could initially fall for an extended period, but a long-term oriented investor wouldn't mind waiting even years for an opportune moment to sell at better prices or never sell at all. In the meantime, they collect income. The classic example is real estate. An increase in real estate market prices is secondary for a long-term real estate investor. They are more concerned about monthly rental income and the stability thereof. In many cases, real estate investors actually prefer lower and falling prices, as to give them the chance to purchase more properties for their growing portfolios. They are only interested in rising real estate prices when they intend to sell; like any financially incentivized gambler would be.

This attitude towards time horizons is a cardinal sign of true investors. Whereas gamblers and speculators are most interested in making money in a hurry, investors don't mind holding quality assets for an indefinite period. They actually wish for it.

There is also the factor of immediate and predictable income. Speculators and gamblers might feel under substantial pressure to generate quick returns or immediate financial rewards, but true investors can wait for different payout scenarios that require longer waiting periods. Their livelihood is not dependent on any one single asset. They have money coming in from their day jobs, real estate portfolios, and other existing investments. Even gold and cash reserves give them a very comfortable financial and psychological advantage.

Full-time gamblers and speculators, on the other hand, don't have that luxury. If they lose or can't play, they don't make money. The same goes for full-time day traders. If markets are closed, they can't earn money. If they have a losing streak for several months, they will certainly feel the pressure. There is the additional factor of debt that needs to be repaid. Speculators tend to be leveraged, adding pressure to perform within a giving time. If they don't, it's game over.

All this gives investors a structural edge and an enormous psychological advantage. They can afford to take better bets with higher chances of winning. These advantages which come at a cost, as we shall later see, give billionaire investors, such as Li Ka-Shing, or Carlos Slim Helú, the mental detachment necessary to cope with uncertain events or even occasional losses. They all follow the same patterns: buying real assets with great income potential with their own financial resources at a time that is very opportune to them. Li Ka-Shing bought real estate and industrial assets in Hong Kong after the British left and everybody believed that Hong Kong was doomed. Carlos Slim purchased prime industrial assets when Mexico experienced its worst recession in a century in 1982. These were all obvious bets, but with higher chances to pay out handsomely and a zero chance of bringing them down completely.

To sum up, what we have learned in this chapter, there are three distinct understandings:

Gambling is when you commit money to predicting the outcome of a certain event, the outcome of which is largely determined by chance. Speculating is when you try to predict the future, particularly price movement. In financial markets, that often means trying to anticipate other player's reactions to particular events. Investing is foremost understanding and purchasing assets at advantageous prices that generate adequate returns and provide sufficient protection for the principal invested. The reactions of others are relevant, but not all-important.

If the differences are clear, and the structural advantages of investing are obvious, why are so many market participants still gambling, rather than investing? Why is it that most participants make terrible bets, still accept terrible odds, and lose money more often than they actually win? Why don't they just follow the examples of successful investors? The only logical explanation for explaining illogical decision-making and behavior must be found in individual psychology. We will find answers in the next chapter.

CHAPTER 5

———◆———

WHY WE TURN INTO GAMBLERS

"It's hard to walk away from a winning streak, even harder to leave the table when you're on a losing one."
—Cara Bertoia

At the beginning of 2007, a wealthy banker asked his maid to come in on a weekend to help out with a social event that he was planning. To his surprise, the maid refused, because she was about to buy her fifth property that weekend. Yes, you read that right. *Fifth*.

He asked her for more details about her wondrous adventure into real estate investing. What he learned astonished him; in her neighborhood, everybody was involved in the real estate game.

Everything was easy, with no-money-down mortgage loans and simple paperwork. She gave him a quick crash course in subprime finance and house flipping. At the end of her lecture, she sheepishly admitted that she would be a millionaire on paper after this deal and that she was considering retirement.

He thanked her and excused her. The moment the maid left, he made some calls. He immediately understood that something was amiss in the financial markets. He called his broker and ordered him to liquidate his stock portfolio over the following days.

In July 2007, only a few months later, the hints of a pending financial disaster appeared when two Bear Stearns Asset Management's flagship real estate subprime mortgage portfolios evaporated into thin air. Soon after, the bank itself collapsed. And, as we now know, that was just the beginning.

How could this have happened? How could something so vast and catastrophic come to pass? What causes people to pour their money into "opportunities" that later turn out to be utterly disastrous, and obviously so, in hindsight? The answer, as always, lies in how humans think and interact.

Market Prices

One of the most interesting examples of psychology and investing converging is the peculiar significance of price quotations, and the dramatic psychological feedback loops these can cause. The very first stock exchange introduced ever-changing price quotations for the shares of the early joint stock companies. Today, electronic quotation boards have lost none of their ancestors' power to mesmerize. They have been a never-ending source of psychological torment for generations of speculators, investors, CEOs, and economic policymakers.

For many CEOs of publicly-listed companies, the power of their own company's stock price quotation is so strong that they have it displayed at key locations within their offices for everyone to see. When Enron (the energy trading company that went bankrupt in 2001) opened its new HQ in Houston, Texas, their stock price quotations were strategically well-placed at the entire new facility—even in their elevators. "We were consumed by it," remembers Amanda Martin Brock, ex-Enron executive. For Kenneth Lay (founder, chairman and CEO) and Jeffrey Skilling (former president, COO, and CEO), their share price quotations were the ultimate symbol of success and testament to their superior strategy.

Prices impose themselves directly on our psyche. When market prices rise, we feel confirmed. When prices drop, we see it as a personal failure. If you've ever found yourself checking your phone for price quotes several times a day, even after trading hours and on the weekend, you'll know what I'm talking about.

Yet, it's perfectly possible to be a successful entrepreneur and not worry about price quotations. Ask any private business owner whose company is not listed on public financial markets how they feel about the price fluctuations of their private businesses. They could not even give you a clear answer of what that price quotation actually may be, let alone the tiny daily fluctuations within it. They might have a general idea of how much they would be willing to sell their businesses for, but they could never pinpoint it with precision. They have a *mental detachment* that allows them to focus on matters that are relevant to their operations, rather than being continuously influenced by price quotations. The same counts for real estate holders. Once you have purchased a property and collected your first rental income, the price quotation for that property becomes irrelevant for many years.

So, then, why the big fuss? What functions do prices have in economies and financial markets, and how do they relate to investing and gambling?

Ideally, investing is a very rational process, free of emotional influences. Although stock prices may have nothing to do with the actual success of business, they are easily accessible and highly visible quantifications of market opinions. Even though on some level, everyone knows market prices are the result of a million variations that may have nothing to do with reality and the tangible world, they still fixate on price quotations as a meaningful reflection of their success. In other words, what we see here is a *rational* thought process being trumped by a *subconscious* desire for validation. And this is the root of a lot of investing behaviors that, in hindsight, make little sense.

The Rational and the Not

Nobel Prize winner Professor Daniel Kahneman of Princeton University researched the human mind: how we make decisions and how we make mistakes. According to Kahneman, "If we think that we have reasons for what we believe, that is often a mistake. Our beliefs, wishes, and hopes are not always anchored in reasons." In his studies, Professor Kahneman and his late colleague Amos Tversky realized that we actually have two systems of thinking. With their research, they opened a new branch of economics called behavioral economics, and with it the sub-category of behavioral finance.

What they described was a world where every one of our decisions and every judgment we make is a result of a battle in our mind—a battle between deep-rooted instincts that manifest themselves through our intuitions. We can compare this with psychoanalyst Sigmund Freud's system of *id* (the deep, beastly, "reptilian" mind), *ego* (the subconscious), and *superego* (provider of moral standards by which the ego operates). In the case of investing, the id is in constant battle with the ego and superego. But whether we call it the "superego" or the "rational brain," there is a part of the mind that you are aware of that is rational, intentional, and complex.

Seth Godin, the famous marketing guru, refers to this as the "lizard brain."[19] It controls our intuitive reactions and many parts of our daily decision making. It has evolved over millions of years into a very powerful control mechanism. It is still present and deeply hidden within all of us, coordinating our most elementary body functions, reflexes, and instincts. Just ask a teenager how often their thoughts stray to sex and you'll see a manifestation of the lizard-brain urge to reproduce. But a feeling tells me not to discriminate young teenage boys.

When Ego Meets Money

Excitement and instant financial rewards are all fine if it works out. The problem comes when we are put under pressure, and our intuitive system has to make critical decisions. Decisions that under normal circumstances should be given more time and processed by our rational system.

According to Kahneman, "our thinking is riddled with systematic mistakes," known among psychologists as *cognitive biases*. The list has constantly grown in number since Daniel Kahneman and Amos Tversky first investigated them: "They make us spend impulsively and be overly influenced by what other people think. They affect our beliefs, our opinions, and our decisions, and we are not even aware it is happening."[20]

When it comes to money, we can immediately recognize some powerful human instincts, such as loss aversion, greed, and preference for immediate rewards. Add the *investor's itch* (the constant need to be active because you might lose out), and you can see that we have a very interesting cocktail of powerful psychological forces that causes various forms of cognitive bias or "human misjudgment." When it comes to making decisions regarding money, it seems that our lizard brain too often takes hold of us, and with some very dire consequences. It seems that we are genetically wired to gamble and speculate over rational, long-term investments.

Gambling and speculating give us instant feedback and reward systems. It induces action that is much more stimulating to our lizard brains than anything else. We know from gambling that all players experience an endorphin rush. When our opioid system is sufficiently stimulated, the release of endorphins is a natural consequence and can lead to the feeling of "being high." In the worst cases, it will even lead to strong forms of addiction. The reverse is also true. We do everything in our power to avoid pain, especially when it involves short-term pain.

When it comes to gambling, we can all agree that any game of money is much more exciting when we have our results as soon as we have placed our bet. For example, betting on rising or falling oil futures today is much more exciting and financially rewarding than keeping a stock for more than five years.The rewards and pains of it are almost instant. It is not unusual for oil prices to fluctuate 3% up or down on any single day. If daily price fluctuations are too small—like in the case of currencies and some larger stocks—you can always lean on financial leverage, that can magnify any potential gains or losses. Add financial derivatives to the trading mix, and market players can easily make up to 10% in minutes rather than years.

In contrast, real investing can be extremely boring. If you invest in either bonds, stocks, or real estate, from the perspective of an investor, it can take months before you get your first income in the form of rent, dividends, or interest. For some long-term investments, it can take years before the financial rewards pan out; i.e., when governments increase their tax and fee revenues from new train lines or airports that they have financed. There is no immediate financial reward. In some cases, the pain caused by the psychological torment of waiting can have a much stronger impact on our opioid system than facing immediate losses. Blaise Pascal, the aforementioned philosopher who gave us probability theory, sums it up in his famous quote, "All man's miseries derive from not being able to sit quietly in a room alone."

Is greed good?

We have developed a natural instinct towards greed. It is without boundaries, gender, or race. In the early days, survival meant having as much food as possible as quickly as possible.

These days, we have plenty of food, but greed has not dissipated. Food has simply been replaced with money and power. Greed is often the main driver in a player's decision making. Some might even argue that envy is the main driver behind greed. Nevertheless, Money is scarce for most of us, and it is still hard controlling an instinct developed over millions of years. Greed is also the force that pushes financial institutions and their henchmen to sell less than appropriate financial products to "gullible investors." It is the force that makes gullible investors buy these products and make them jump on the bandwagon with total disregard for common sense, scrutiny, or the simplest form of due diligence. But, it's not only greed that leads us into decisions that we might later regret.

Fear of loss

Loss aversion is a person's tendency "to strongly prefer avoiding losses to acquiring gains." According to Kahneman, we feel the pain of a loss much more than we feel the pleasure of a gain. Most studies suggest that losses are psychologically twice as powerful as gains. If you lose $10 today, you feel terrible. But, if you find $10 tomorrow, you will not be as pleased with your luck as someone who found the same amount without previously losing it. From your perspective, you're not as lucky as the person who found $10, because you've already lost $10. This aversion to loss leads to risk aversion.

A country that uniformly celebrates risk aversion is Japan. Their experiences with bubbles and economic stagnation have marked several generations of Japanese so much that they prefer to keep their cash stashed under mattresses, swearing never to return to financial markets. It might take several more generations to get it out of their collective system, but bankers and financiers are continually working on this, so that the "great forgetting" can finally set in. *The great forgetting* is a term popularized by Daniel Quinn referring to civilizations that are doomed to repeat the mistakes of the past.

The Herd Instinct

When it comes to the Japanese and the financial markets, there is another crucial example of a powerful cognitive bias called "social proof." Social conformity is very strong in Japan and at times takes on very interesting and peculiar forms. But it's not only the Japanese who display a strong form of social proof. We all have a herd instinct in us. We feel affirmed in our choice to buy when everyone else is buying and feel very uneasy holding our assets when everybody is selling. The herd instinct works as an amplifier for many other cognitive biases, particularly fear and greed. In a crowd, it's much more difficult to suppress the urges of greed or the shivers of fear that capture us all.

The Rearview Mirror

A classic human misjudgment when it comes to money and gambling is what is known in casino terms as gambler's fallacy: "the belief that the chances of something happening with a fixed probability become higher or lower as the process is repeated." People who fall for it believe that past events affect the probability of something happening in the future. An example is when a gambler at the roulette table bets his or her money on red simply because red hasn't been drawn for multiple rounds. Casino operators happily publish their past plays of red and black occurrences or even and odd numbers for gamblers to see. Unfortunately, neither dice nor roulette balls have a memory and past patterns really mean nothing.

For investors, speculators, and the entire industry, there is something similar to the gambler's fallacy. It is what Warren Buffett calls the "looking into the rearview mirror" phenomenon. According to Buffett: "(...) investor's projected out into the future what they were seeing. That's their unshakable habit: looking into the rear-view mirror instead of through the windshield." In other words, what market players have observed in the immediate past is automatically projected into the future. This applies not only to earnings and price forecasts but also to risk calculations and economic forecasts that rely on a similar set of data. This type of fallacy is so common within the professional community that it ensnares leading central banks and academia. It was this fallacy that led to the subprime crisis between 2007 and 2008; people assumed that because house prices had risen for a number of years, they would continue to rise.

Another interesting consequence of that fallacy is that it applies to both bull (rising market) and bear (falling or stagnant market) conditions. When one of the worst bear markets in United States history held sway between 1964 to 1981, all sorts of professional projections were made. They truly believed that the dire situation would continue for several years into the future. The result was that the majority of retail and professional market participants missed the biggest and longest bull market America had ever seen. As of 2016, we seem to be in reverse; there seems to be a strong, powerful notion that the prevailing market conditions of the past bull market, (built on the majors stock market indices' historical data in 1982), will endure. The market consensus is that the recent past performance averages can be easily projected into the future. That particularly applies to U.S. stock market averages that are projected to yield continuous 6 to 8% returns annually. They will very soon learn their own lessons on the rear-view fallacy.

Authority Misguidance

On of the most powerful and dangerous biases of all—and with serious personal consequences—is the bias related to false and misled authority. Blind obedience is sometimes a way to rationalize foolish actions. Based on Munger's observations, "We tend to obey an authority, especially when we are uncertain, supervised or when people around us are doing the same. We are most easily influenced by credible authorities, those we see as both knowledgeable and trustworthy. Names and reputation influences us. And symbols of power or status like titles, possessions, rank uniforms, or a nice suit and tie."[21] This goes as far as associating complexity and incomprehension with authority and sophistication. Sometimes, we are overly impressed by something that simply sounds clever, even though we don't understand them. Another example is when famous people endorse products, even though they do not use the products or services that they endorse. Even worse is that today anyone can call themselves an expert by simply rigging the system. Tim Ferriss, in his iconic book *The 4-Hour Workweek*, gave a blueprint on how anyone can become a respectable authority with a few simple steps in a matter of days. Voilà, people listen and follow.

Lollapalooza Tendency

The term "Lollapalooza Tendency" was coined by Charlie Munger in a famous speech at Harvard University.[22] He defines it as "the tendency to get extreme consequences from confluences of psychological tendencies acting in favor of a particular outcome." What that means is that cognitive biases seldom operate in a vacuum independently from each other. Instead, for any decision, we might have several biases working congruently in one direction causing a *snapping effect* in our brains.

What does this mean for individual investors? In their decision-making process, whether buying or selling, it is never only our logical brain that is responsible for each decision. Social proof and loss aversion have as much importance in one decision as "authority-misinfluences" and over-optimism.

Women and Investing

According to a research report by Fidelity Investments, women seem to be better savers than men. Their study showed that while men save 7.9% of their salaries, women save 8.3%. Over time, this small difference has a big impact on potential wealth accumulation.

The report also suggests that women are better investors as well. Terrance Odean and Brad Barber, who conducted the research, found "that women outperform men annually by about one percentage point." According to them, one possible reason for this is that "women are less inclined to check their portfolios... and they change their asset allocation less frequently than male investors." "When women do invest, they do better," says Kathleen Murphy of President of Fidelity Personal Investing. "But too many women don't."[23]

From my experience observing female investors, I always had the impression they are less emotionally invested in the investment decision process than men. For male investors, investing seems to be a matter of pride and personal self-esteem. They see it as a competitive game where making prudent investment decisions is secondary, but beating their peers is a priority. Their over-competitiveness leads them to take higher risks and lower their guard for smooth talking advisors that usually ends in purely speculative bets.

However, women are not free of cognitive biases. Again, Japan offers an interesting case study. In Japan, where homemakers traditionally manage the family's budget, Japanese have, on average, done very well for themselves financially. In their culture, many husbands are known for spending their money on drinks with their colleagues, trips to the race tracks, and Pachinko parlors. Under the careful but rigid leadership of the dominant homemaker, most Japanese families still consider themselves middle class with a conservative attitude and emphasis on traditional education and classic cultural development. This attitude has always been reflected in their private investment operations symbolized by the stereotypical homemaker.

Even financially savvy Japanese homemakers have not been free of psychological misguidance in the form of herd mentality or authority-misinfluences. When opinionated leaders touted stocks and real estate until the bitter end of the Japanese Bubble economy, many households contributed to the bubble madness. In the dreadful post-bubble era, nearly everyone became ultra-conservative, preferring cash to any other investment opportunity.

Then, when families felt pressured by a new world of ultra-low interest rates on their savings, many female investors engaged in "yen carry trade." According to Investopedia, "The carry trade is a form of speculation in which investors borrow a low-cost currency like the yen and buy high-growth currency, netting a profit. In recent years, for example, Japanese housewifes began accumulating Australian dollar deposits, which yielded a significantly higher rate than they could get at home."

The investment rationale was to buy higher interest yielding currency (for example, Australian dollars that yielded 5%), by exchanging Japanese Yen that yielded almost nothing. Most of Japan was not concerned with currency rate fluctuations, as long as they could cash in the dividends from their international investments. Besides, during this period, the Japanese yen was consistently weakening, giving them capital gains when they exchanged their foreign currencies back into yen. (They received more yen than they had initially invested). Convinced by the logic and reaffirmed by female opinion leaders, hordes of Japanese homemakers joined the trend and became a force to be reckoned with in currency markets. According to the Bank of Japan in 2007, Japanese homemakers' trading activity helped stabilize the currency markets because of their tendency to buy on dips and sell into rallies.

What began as a conservative money making opportunity quickly turned into an orgy of currency speculation that ended in 2008 with horrendous losses. A significant amount of this trading was carried out through online margin accounts, which offered leverage of 20 to 100 times. Because it was so easy to do and highly encouraged by Japan's opinion leaders, Japanese investment banks and brokers hired more female role models to encourage their clients to trade and to make use of easy financial leverage.

When the Japanese yen suddenly strengthened, in the wake of the subprime crisis, their yen trade collapsed. With their over-leveraged positions, many families lost the household savings that they had been amassing for many years in savings and trades. To make matters worse, their delicate stock market portfolios collapsed at the same time.

According to Noriko Hama, an economist at Kyoto's Doshisha University Business School, in a Financial Times interview in 2009, "I tend to think the Mrs. Watanabes [i.e., 'Mrs. Joneses'] have been silly. They got carried away by this wind of savings to investment, this idea that financial wizardry is the thing of the 21st century. IT banking and FX trading; all of these things came at them and they were swept off their feet."[24]

Nevertheless, female investors seem to have a failsafe system embedded in their decision-making when it comes to managing their household money. They tend to follow their risk-averse instincts much more often than their male counterparts. Combined with the previously mentioned factors, women, on average, make better investors.

Every aspiring and seasoned investor needs to understand that when it comes to making decisions concerning money, every decision is as much determined by rational parameters as it is by non-rational factors: our lizard brain and cognitive biases, as well as theories, models, and mathematical formulas. We can see the link and transformation about why investing can quickly become speculation. If all three forms are in some way betting money on the future and dealing with uncertainty, human inclination tends to lean towards the easiest form of action, even if we don't understand the deeper ramifications of each small bet we make. Wall Street has long recognized the inner conflicts of each player and has found ways to exploit those conflicts. In the next chapter, we will take a closer look at Wall Street's financial incentives and why we are encouraged to be speculators and gamblers.

CHAPTER 6

———•◆•———

WALL STREET AND CASINOS

"The most dangerous untruths are truths slightly distorted."
—George C. Lichtenberg

E ver wondered what Wall Street folks do in their free time? They gamble!

Gambling culture is rampant on and off Wall Street. Financial workers love going on the occasional weekend tour to Atlantic City or Las Vegas. If they don't gamble in casinos, they speculate and trade for their own accounts in currencies, stocks and derivatives. Wall Street has been trying to shut down this practice, due to an obvious conflict of interest. It seems there hasn't been much success thus far.

These are the people who control *the money game* and who want us to play it. We need to look at their financial incentives, and how they profit from and take advantage of an imperfect system with imperfect players. They are a hybrid group that is part game facilitator/part proxy/part player made up of investment banks, brokers, money managers, and henchmen. Wall Street institutions are terrible money managers for their clients and terrible investments for their shareholders but have managed to create a system that keeps generating enormous sums of money for themselves, provided they can keep cash moving through it.

Fee Incomes and Attracting Customers

In a recent interview at Berkshire Hathaway's annual shareholders meeting, Warren Buffett said this about Wall Street's money-making capability:

"There's been far, far, far more money made by people in Wall Street through salesmanship abilities than through investment abilities..."

This observation is certainly true. The majority of Wall Street works in back offices, IT departments, and sales and marketing divisions. They range from the foot soldiers at rural sales offices to professional account managers in M&A (Mergers & Acquisitions) departments in Manhattan. Only a few people make their living through investment decisions, and the majority do an unsatisfactory job for their clients. They regularly fail to beat their benchmarks or add value for the fees they charge. According to the Financial Times, "86% of active equity funds underperform."[25] Investing directly in banks and investment banks is not a walk in the park either. As a matter of fact, they are usually appalling investments for their shareholders. In an almost predictable fashion, they disappoint and demand new capital, diluting existing shareholders interest.

To give a short, illustrative example of a Wall Street firm's failure and its appalling investment track record, consider the case of Deutsche Bank, a global commercial and investment bank with asset and wealth management departments. When announcing a €6.2 billion ($7 billion)[26] write off for the quarter ending October 2015, they revealed some staggering losses from proprietary trading (trading for themselves) and write-offs from past strategic investments, such as acquiring Banker's Trust (purchased for $10.1 billion way back in 1998). They might all be accounting gimmicks, but since 2008, they have made three capital increases of about €17 billion ($17 billion) in total. Since 2012, they have also periodically declared giant losses of over €10 billion ($11.3 billion) with some meager earnings in between. Since 2015, their stock price has lost more than 50% of their value. Even worse, Deutsche Bank's constant battle with the law became a permanent financial burden. The bank has had to make several provisions for ongoing legal skirmishes with financial regulators, which amounted to $1.4 billion in 2016.

Deutsche Bank is not alone in this situation; a string of investment and management failures have rippled through the industry. Leading banks like Royal Bank of Scotland, UBS, and Citigroup come to mind. For their shareholders, that means having to be on standby to provide fresh capital when management messes up. If that isn't sufficient or shareholders resist, there are still central banks and governments that are prepared to bail them out. Their largest shareholders are usually pension funds, endowment funds, insurances companies, and asset management companies, which I am sure you already have a financial interest in.

Still, Wall Street has created the most wondrous money-making machine the world has ever seen. No other industry pays higher average salaries and grants, as well as huge bonus payments. The pay ratio of compensation and benefits to net revenues of an investment bank like Goldman Sachs is around 40%. In 2015, Goldman Sachs's compensation amount was about $13 billion, with 37,000 employees on the payroll.[27] No other industry has become as important to our economic system while contributing so little to the economic prosperity of society. It's a cash cow that keeps on giving for those participants who understand how to milk the cow.

So, how did the big players acquire their colossal riches? And how do they continue to stay on top?

To begin with, there is one thing you need to remember: there is almost no way to play *the money game* without going through Wall Street. The gatekeepers of the financial market are brokers, commercial banks, and giant investment banks. Together, they control armies of salespeople, entire product categories and markets. They collect fees and huge amounts of data from their clients and other financial institutions. They deal at the highest level with the largest money managers and even governments. They control and partly own exchanges and electronic settlement systems. They own shares in the Federal Reserve and are members of its money-clearing system. They influence financial regulations through massive lobbying activities and, therefore, the rules of the financial games we play today. A testimony of their power and influence can even be seen in the architecture they sponsor. More than 2000 years ago, we saw monuments built for gods that could be seen from the far reaches of any city. Today, when we enter the most dominant cities in the world, the first thing we recognize are the banking towers in the distance. That says something about the gods we worship today.

With power over the system, the biggest financial institutions in the world and their often brilliant employees, have set about to create an elaborate network of products and mechanisms that provide two key incentives: 1) people playing the system need to make more money 2) people outside the system must start playing.

A lucrative business model

If we look closely, we can identify the two main revenue sources on Wall Street.

1. Fee income: the most vital, stable and recurrent source of income.
2. House bets: the secondary revenue model is based on lucrative house bets

Fee income has very low risk and is relatively easy to manage.

It might require an elaborate sales distribution network and marketing staff to coordinate themselves. But once this dream factory starts running smoothly, financial institutions can move up a gear or two, and money will flow in. Whenever money flows from A to B, there is a possibility to take a cut. Their primary goal is to convince clients to play and stay in the money game at all costs, which encourages their business traffic and increases trading volume. Then, they move on to collect their fee income, which represents the building block of all those famous bonus pools.

This system is not very different from a casino business model. In casinos, it's not a secret that they operate on simple principles. It's a big numbers game, and the house always wins. The more people that enter a casino, the more money can flow. The more games they play, the higher the chance that the casino takes all of their money. As Nicky Santoro explained in the movie Casino (1995), "...in casinos, the cardinal rule is to keep them playing and keep them coming back—the longer they play, the more they lose, in the end, we get it all."

There are some eye-opening parallels between legalized gambling and playing the financial markets:

- Casinos lure you in with either free or relatively low-investment games. Slot machines or simple card games draw in millions of new players. Wall Street's financial institutions see to it that even their youngest clients get a taste of the stock markets. Today, many banks invite their young and potential future clients to take part in "harmless" stock market games with fictitious money.
- At casinos, many players don't know the details of the games—the exact rules, tricks and probabilities involved in every single bet they place. Even fewer know the games well enough to play them successfully. Likewise, potential new investors read everything that is promoted by the financial media and Wall Street but don't really understand the core principles of chance and prudent money management. They get lost in investing strategies, trading

screens, rumors, and financial jargon. They miss the most what's important—not to lose money.

- Have you ever seen a trading desk at an online broker or trading floor? They're big, blinking screens with red and green flashes and banners scrolling with screens changing every second. Add to these intra-day and long-term charts and you feel like you're at the racetrack or in front of Pachinko slot machines.

- Casinos tend to celebrate their few winners with loud sirens and music. They provide the instant feedback and the encouragement that other players need. Financial markets don't have to do this. The financial media and winners do it for them. It's just like when your neighbor brags about his latest stock market gains or when celebrity money managers talk about making another $1 billion in winnings for their clients. It all seems so simple and easy.

- If you search "top winning gambling strategies," you get over 29 million hits. You will get a list of possible winning gambling strategies, all with a high level of confidence, which makes winning in gambling sound like a certainty. The financial industry uses the same techniques. They bombard us with investments and trading strategies, and with courses and books that seem to make sure that you are the only winner.

- Casinos are open 24/7. By letting gamblers play at all hours of the day and through the night, casinos increase their odds of winning. In the same way, online brokers today offer worldwide trading in currencies, stocks and commodities, trading happens for almost 24 hours each day. You could trade Japanese yen in the late evening, buy some European stocks in the morning, and end your day with some gold commodities trading, only to repeat the entire cycle the next day.

The Sweet Lies

As we've seen above, it is crucial to the Wall Street system that there remain money pouring in and enough stimuli for their clients. The gatekeepers of the finance industry would argue that all of this is essential to keep money flowing around the world and delivering capital to where it is needed. As industry insiders say, "You can pay us to decide how your money is used, because we know best!" For this to work, we need efficient propaganda with a mix of half-truths, lies, and a lot of complexity, the basis for all their sales pitches. What follows are the most common and widely promoted lies.

Lie 1: Investing means stock markets, now!

The most worrisome notion about modern investing today is the automatic association with stock markets and fund investment. When you ask a random person on the street about investing, they will come up with answers that likely involves stocks, funds, or Wall Street. The notion is that when you have cash, it needs to be invested in financial products promoted by Wall Street. A growing majority of retail investors insist that they need to put their money immediately "to work," and it should work *all the time*. Somehow, the general public is convinced that investing equals Wall Street. From Wall Street's perspective, it makes a lot of sense. An inactive person with a lot of cash outside the money game is the worst client; so, they tell you that holding cash is bad, and that investing means buying stocks, funds and promising financial products.

For the majority of human history, many people got wealthy—a few fabulously so—without stepping inside a stock exchange. Less than 70 years ago, today's highly touted form of investing had no relevance to the general public. For many, financial market investing became mainstream because of Ronald Reagan's new economic policies. In industrialized countries such as Germany, it didn't matter until the mid-90s, because it was the domain of a few enterprising individuals and wealthy family offices. Germans who didn't invest in stocks and funds did very well for themselves. Yes, the general public has always purchased fixed income securities, short-term money papers or bank certificates, but that is nothing compared to the financial product variety we face today and the enormous outside pressure to play the game. Consider the case of Japan, one of the top five economies in the world with a strong middle class. After 1990, many of the Japanese completely lost their enthusiasm for stock and fund investing, as it marked their financial armageddon—Japan's massive real estate and stock market bubble popped. Until fairly recently, the largest pension fund in the world, the Government Pension Investment Fund (GPIF) of Japan, with about $1.1 trillion assets under management, didn't have a single stock position in its portfolio mix.

Only through massive market manipulation, at the highest governmental levels, has stock investing seen a somewhat lukewarm revival among Japanese individual investors. Today, economists estimate that the Japanese central bank, the Bank of Japan (BOJ), is the largest shareholder of Japan's publicly listed companies through massive purchases in Japanese Exchange Traded Funds (ETF).[28] In effect, Japan's government and the BOJ are gamblers with a massive all-in bet to stimulate stock market investments among the Japanese retail clients. If the bet doesn't work out, its whole population will pay the bill.

The truth is the general public does not need to participate in Wall Street's games. Millions of Germans have done well for their retirement without ever having invested in stocks or funds. Generations of Japanese have done well for themselves and their retirement plans by just keeping their cash under their pillow or keeping it in gold and real estate. There are other ways to take care of your retirement needs that range from saving more to establishing small businesses or maintaining working opportunities beyond the set retirement age. Remember: no matter what the publicity machine says, you do not *have* to invest in stocks or funds to make money "work" for you.

Lie 2: Money Lies in Trends

Another way Wall Street tries to get people to commit their money is by identifying what they believe to be cast-iron trends, then monetizing those. It's common knowledge that we are better off at investing in something that experiences growth and future potential. There are always a few trends that are more or less guaranteed to become reality. In investing parlance, they have a tailwind. For example:

- People live longer.
- There is an expansion of renewable energies.
- Robotics and AI (artificial intelligence) will become more widespread.

Many books have been written on the topic of investing in future technologies, research, and science. Large venture capital funds have made it their specialty to fund future technologies and promising projects.

Unfortunately, most industries trends and visionary predictions have been a financial grave for many. There are neither protections for the capital invested nor indications of any types of stable returns that make their investment worthwhile. On the contrary, further funding is usually required, as the initial capital invested is frequently insufficient. The investor is usually presented with the classic investor's dilemma of having to throw good money after bad or risk losing the entire initial investment. This should not keep people away from opening their purses to these noble endeavors, but they should be clear that their money is considered a donation rather than a real investment for future wealth.

A good example of the perils of investing in fads and popular trends is the car and airline industry. How much money was lost financing all of those early car companies that don't exist anymore? How much money was lost financing new airline companies at the beginning of the 20th century, and then a few decades later, restructuring a few remaining airline companies? The large majority of investors in both industries have very little to show, yet they were the trendiest investments of their time. Similar scenarios have occurred with other revolutionary technologies, such as the TV or dotcom companies. The majority of investors, particularly those who came a little late to the party, lost huge amounts of money, even though all of the experts' forecasts came to fruition.

This doesn't only apply to whole industries, but to financial products themselves, such as theme funds and exotic-sounding structured products. When BRIC funds (Brazil, Russia, India, & China) became mainstream among retail investors and everyone had to have one in their portfolios, the real winners were the first movers who invested early on at very favorable prices. By the time the masses invested, early investors were preparing themselves to cash out with very generous capital gains. Those a bit late to the party picked up the check. In 2015, the once iconic BRIC fund folded and merged with another Emerging Market Fund, due to several years of appalling performances. Guess who the losers were? As of the writing of this book, trendy investments themes include investing in VR (Virtual Reality) or AI (Artificial Intelligence) technology or single companies such as UBER, Snapchat or AirBnB. Though not publicly listed, these three companies have already reached jaw-dropping valuations that could be right out of a fairytale from the land of flying unicorns. Yes, a few investors will make lots of money—staggering amounts of money—but it won't be you or the masses of naive followers. Trend and fashion investors would be well-advised to heed Peter Lynch's observation: "It's a real tragedy when you buy a stock that's overpriced, the company is a big success, and still you don't make any money."[29]

Lie 3: The Gospel of Diversification

To keep people invested at all times, though aware that nervous folks worry about price volatility and crashes, Wall Street has found the perfect solution: the gospel of diversification. The theory behind it is that when owning or allocating your cash to a set of asset classes—e.g. stock, bonds, and real estate—diversifying your holdings can protect you from the ups and downs of today's erratic markets. The idea is that you can stay invested and tolerate the price volatility of individual asset classes while hoping to reap market returns. Of course, all fees are charged, whether they perform or not.

Another argument for extensive asset allocation is that if you own all possible assets spanning the entire globe, it will enable you to participate in any hot asset class. If Chinese stocks are hot, you will have some exposure; if oil or gold are hot, you will have some exposure. So, retail investors get to play the hot games of the big guys through diversification.

To make things even more surreal; you can diversify within asset classes. Professional advice is supposed to navigate the naïve investor through the minefields of asset class selection, but will also assist in selecting the best funds and managers. Professional advice, as a result, comes in two layers: on the top, clients need advice on selecting the hottest, trendiest asset class and the best fund managers within those classes. On the second level, clients have to pay managers for selecting the best investment in each asset class—that includes the growing number of index funds and ETFs. So, you pay advisors to select a team of fund managers and you pay fund managers to select the best securities. You could potentially add a financial planner, private banker, or tax consultant as the fees accumulate. It is a wonderful business model that generates continuous trading commissions and advisory fees in the name of risk diversification.

An average investor, who follows the standard advice today, will end up with at least three to five different funds or a fund of funds (funds that invest in several funds managed by other companies). It's been estimated that an average retail investor with $50,000 to spare would end up with at least a 1,000 stocks in their portfolio and a similar or even larger amount of bonds. Congratulations! You have just won the prize for being the most diversified retail investor with guaranteed average performance... and front seats in the next financial crisis.

The bottom line is this: over-diversification has nothing to do with prudent investing or appropriate risk management. It neither guarantees long-term performance nor protects investors from market extreme variances such as those experienced during the subprime crises.

Diversification doesn't protect you from overvalued purchases, regardless of the number of purchases. With any diversification, you can still very much overpay and lose substantial amounts of money. As Joe Ponzio, a former broker and trader, eloquently explained, "Extensive diversification, merely for the sake of diversification, is downright stupid."[30]

To be clear, intelligent diversification makes sense. As a matter of a fact, you can diversify as much as you'd like, but the timing and reasoning for your diversification matter. If you bought all of the assets in the world with funds diversified into the hundreds at the peak of 2007, no diversification on this planet would have saved you from very sizeable losses. According to experts, it will be fine in the long run. Maybe, after ten years, you will have made up your losses, all the while being charged annual fees at all levels. Some hardened Japanese investors from the early 1990s are still hoping for a miraculous recovery of their well-diversified portfolios. They have been waiting for more than 20 years.

Lie 4: Wall Street Knows Best

Joe Ponzio states, "The brokerage firms and mutual funds that control Wall Street and the markets want you to believe that investing is too hard and too dangerous to do on your own. They also tell you that it's not possible to beat the returns of the general stock market."[31] As contradictory as it may seem, this is where Wall Street steps in. They are the professionals. They know all the tips and tricks and urge you to hand your money over to them.

They forget to mention only one thing. Making side bets on gamblers or speculators is not investing, but gambling. Do they use their advantages for their clients or themselves?

If you hand over your money to some professional poker players in Las Vegas, there is a high chance that you'll lose all of your money. Believe it or not, the same counts on Wall Street. We've seen that most professional Wall Street players speculate and trade, rather than invest long-term. And most of them stink at it. If you put your money with brokers and fund managers who trade, speculate, and make big bets on currencies, commodities, or stocks on your behalf, then it is not an investment, but a disguised form of gambling. It might go well, but it might also end up in a complete loss. The question is, where's the line between a good money manager from a dud? To exacerbate things, finding one who is committed to invest, and not gambling, is time-consuming. Finding someone who is honest and takes care of your interests before their own is like finding the needle in a haystack. When people invested in Buffett's early partnership in Omaha back in 1956, it was pure luck. For them, it was a simple bet on Warren Buffett the person, not the investment manager and capital allocator we know today. They were extremely lucky to have met him early on. There was not a single German, French, or Japanese investor in the early partnerships, and even some of Buffett's own friends and acquaintances refused to invest.

And what about the thousands of fund failures and scams that we never hear of due to a phenomenon called survivor bias or survival bias? It describes "a logical error of concentrating on the people or things that "survived" some process and inadvertently overlooking those that did not because of their lack of visibility." This can lead to false conclusions in several different ways. Today's investors simply forget or ignore the countless cases where investors lost money trusting their friends and family. They invest in the unknown and new fund managers and funds. We give them the benefit of the doubt because they certainly had good intentions and moral principles. But for some reason, they fail because of bad timing, back luck, or incompetence, losing trillions worth of investors' capital. We will never hear of them unless they are worthy of headline news.

In the face of these obvious risks and challenges for finding the right advisors and fund manager, wouldn't it be easier, cheaper, and riskier to invest in your own business, local real estate or in the businesses well-known by you?

Lie 5: "Stable Income"

There is this strong desire among professional and amateur investors to have a fixed income like stable monthly investment returns. They dream of this perfect passive income comparable to monthly salaries, stock dividends, and stock market returns that secure their owners a safe and financially stable life. They are constantly working on finding the latest financially-engineered magical product that promises to deliver with disclaimers longer than the actual sales pamphlet.

Over the last 20 years, several investment products presented themselves to investors for their sophisticated risk-adjusted returns with almost predictable monthly returns. It usually sounds as if they have invented a secret formula for turning lead into gold. The patterns are always the same. For many years in a row, they present their investors with catchy monthly returns of 1 to 2% with almost zero mathematical risk of losing. These are truly wondrous products as long as they last, but they blow up and the money is lost. The last time it didn't work out was after the subprime crisis, when a few German banks in Düsseldorf, and other naive clients around the world, went belly up. Apparently, they fell for these products but didn't read or understand the disclaimer. If it sounds too good to be true, it usually is.

Key Takeaways

In the second part, we have seen the fundamental differences between purely taking chances, speculating, and investing. We have also seen the elements that unify them all—the placement of money on an uncertain future. In many ways, participating in financial markets shows remarkable similarities to gambling at casinos. The fundamental similarities, the flow of money, the games we can play, the information flow, and the subtle appeal to human shortcomings are obvious.

We have seen how anyone can easily turn from an investor into a simple gambler succumbing to their own cognitive biases that could cost them dearly. The worst thing is that Wall Street is designed to stimulate those cognitive biases in each player. It is an entire industry of third parties, commercial banks, and investment banks feeding into a system of confusion and misinformation to stimulate the flow of money from A to B. While this happens, fees come their way. We have seen that there is another, more sinister reason, why Wall Street wants you to play and participate in *the money game* at all times.

In a casino, you have fixed rules and it is transparent what can and cannot be done. In theory, the same fundamental principle should apply to all financial institutions that promote themselves to serve their clients and uphold their fiduciary duties. But this is where the casino comparison stops and the second revenue model of Wall Street institutions comes into play. Wall Street operators have gotten used to playing with house money. They take a few bets for themselves and diversify their business model, which results in some dire consequences for the rest of the players.

In the third and final part of this book, I will present some key observations that show that playing the money game is a losing proposition right from the start for the average investor. Wall Street might not have the same edge that casinos enjoy, but they have always had the resourcefulness to create their own edge.

In the meantime, you should decide, if you like what you are being told by the game facilitators. You should remember the following simple **DONTs**:

- Don't automatically assume that investing means stock markets, funds and Wall Street.
- Don't fall into the trap that your own capital needs to be working for you at all times, especially on other people's terms.
- Don't fall for theme or trend investing ploys.
- Don't become a gambler yourself, by betting on other gamblers.
- Don't buy something for the sake of diversification.
- Don't believe stories of safe, stable, and predictable investment income.

PART III

THE DARK SIDE

CHAPTER 7

---◆---

FORGING THE EDGE

"Victorious warriors win first and then go to war, while defeated warriors go to war first and then seek to win."
—Sun Tzu

The best strategy for any professional poker player is either to play for really big prize money and prestige (such as taking part in the World Series of Poker) or play amateurs and patsies and make easy money from mistakes and misjudgments by less sophisticated players. There is a famous scene in the movie *Rounders* (1998) where star poker player Matt Damon sits down at a poker table in Atlantic City aimed at tourists; he knows half of the players at the table by name. However, they all pretend to be amateurs and draw in one unassuming tourist after another.

The movie beautifully depicts the happy faces that join the games and the despair when the gullible players with empty pockets. They never knew what hit them.

Imagine the croupier in a large casino at a blackjack table, a person, who with the protection of the casino management, bets on his own position or on the position of one of his gambling clients. He plays this game, backed by house money, day in and out. Not only is he allowed to count cards, but he is actually encouraged to do so; all the while serving cards to customers. He is encouraged to pick out just the best bets with the best possible payouts. In the long term, guess who makes more money—the player or the croupier?

The financial industry is also like this. They have their finger on the pulse of financial markets, and they have the highest incentives to find either inefficiencies or weaknesses in the financial system. Companies have dedicated "prop desks" where "prop trading" takes place. "Prop" is short for proprietary trading—industry jargon for "trading with your own money instead of your clients." But technically, this is the wrong definition. They *always* play with other people's money, as prop traders trade with the funds their shareholders and creditors entrust to them. The easiest way to understand prop desks and proprietary trading is to see them as internal *hedge funds*—funded, owned and controlled by an investment bank's top management. How Wall Street institutions turned into giant trading floors, their similarity, and bonds with hedge funds and how they profit from them will be discussed in this chapter.

Hedge Funds—Searcher for Patsies

You might have heard stories about George Soros (credited with "breaking" the Bank of England in 1992) and John Paulson (who profited from the subprime collapse to the tune of $4bn by predicting it and betting that it would happen). They were both hedge fund managers, as were Benjamin Graham and many of his peers and disciples. So what, exactly, is a hedge fund, and what makes it different to all the other pots of money out there?

The term goes back to 1949. Alfred Winslow Jones, a sociologist and former Fortune magazine writer, started an investment pool that he called a "hedged fund." "When Jones liked a stock, he would borrow money to buy more of it. The leverage increased his profits and risk. To counter the risk, Jones sold short stocks that he felt were overpriced. This was "hedging" the fund's bets. Jones called the leverage and short-selling "speculative tools used for conservative ends."[32]

Today's hedge funds don't really hedge nor are they considered safe investments. They are simply legal entities that allow for the management of money for other people, without falling under rigid financial regulation mutual funds or other institutional money managers fall under that cater to the "unsophisticated masses." They can bet money on whatever they like, as long as it is OK with their investors and financial backers. Hedge funds have always been reserved for individuals with lots of money and professional investors—the sophisticated or smart money you might call them.

Hedge funds are usually the most aggressive and most incentivized players on Wall Street. They receive their usual annual management fee in advance ranging from 1% to 2% of the assets they manage, plus a 20% cut from all gains they make in a year. If you consider their business model from a slightly different angle, hedge fund managers are de facto borrowers who use their client's money as financial leverage, but get paid for it generously. If they lose their clients" money for clients, they are protected by law, as they are usually structured in limited liability companies. Not a bad business model.

However, with this comes all the moral complications that unusual excessive cash payouts have on highly intelligent and less morally inclined players: ranging from excessive risk-taking to very aggressive business practices (just to maximize their own financial payouts). A few are not afraid to challenge central banks, especially when they work together in packs. Some of them are $20 billion in size or bigger, and the largest hedge funds are so big that they deploy several hedge fund strategies at the same time. They can even defy entire nations, like when Elliott Management Corporation (EMC), led by Paul Singer, forced the government of Argentina to negotiate terms for some of its outstanding debt. Singer bought a large number of Argentinian sovereign bonds during that country's default in 2001—and then refused to let the Argentinian government get away without paying them what was due by the original, pre-default terms of the bonds. To show that EMC means business, EMC went so far as to confiscate an Argentine naval training vessel that lay anchored at the coast of Ghana in October 2012. In March 2016, the Argentinian government, EMC and three more hedge funds agreed to a deal that would end a more than decade-long legal battle.

Hedge funds are designed to make money in every market condition, whether bear or bull, slow or fast. They have models and strategies to profit from any inefficiencies they can detect. Now, you may be wondering what exactly "inefficiency" means. In an investing context, "inefficiency" refers to the failure of people in the market to properly capitalize on the opportunities presented to them. More practically, we're talking about things like overpaying and undervaluing stocks and not understanding the mathematical correlations between them. All situations give rise to the possibility that someone does know the real price profiting. It's in the interest of savvy investors, banks, and hedge funds to have masses of uninformed people in the market, throwing their money around and jumping on any investment fad they can get their hands on.

How these institutions capitalize on such inefficiencies will stagger you. Below, we'll examine three of the most dramatic and effective strategies: the rise of the "quants," betting in "bots," and "fat-tail" players.

Ed Thorp and the Rise of the Quants

The story of Edward O. Thorp should be read and studied by any aspiring investor, as it demonstrates the interconnection of professional gambling and speculation that ultimately leads to the logical consequences for intelligent investing. Thorp was one of the pioneers of hedge funds and early representative of Quant hedge funds, a highly mathematical approach to investing. In the early 1970s, Thorp, former math professor, master blackjack player, and retired professional hedge fund manager, got an invitation from actor Paul Newman to discuss a possible investment in his hedge fund Princeton/Newport Partners. Newman had just done *The Sting*. (The plot involves him teaming up with Robert Redford to con one of the most notorious Chicago gangsters in a horse racing bet.) Thorp had a beer with Newman on the Twentieth Century Fox lot. Newman knew about Thorp's career as a blackjack player and asked how much Thorp could make at blackjack if he did it full-time. Thorp answered $300,000 a year.

"Why aren't you out there doing it?" Newman asked.

"Would you do it?" Thorp answered.

Thorp knew from his personal research that Newman must have made about $6 million that year—an amount similar to what he was then earning at his hedge fund. After a serious but friendly discussion, Newman decided not to invest with Princeton-Newport because he felt uncomfortable with the way hedge funds tried to minimize taxes.[33]

Thorp didn't really need Newman's money for his hedge fund, he had other investors in his fund. According to William Poundstone, author of *Fortune's Formula*, one investor was a former Warren Buffett client, who invested in the early Buffett Partnerships before it was closed. He had Warren Buffett himself check out Ed Thorp at a personal dinner event at his house in Omaha. They both hit it off and Warren Buffett gave the green light to his friend to invest in Ed Thorp's hedge fund. He wouldn't regret it.[34]

Thorp had always been fascinated with numbers and how to make money. He was in search of the perfect money-making formula. With his math skills and extensive research in the field of gambling, he devised a betting strategy that was based on calculating the odds of each bet. He used early computers to run a variety of calculations and simulations for his bankroll, and came up with the optimized blackjack play, which he named his "Basic Strategy." He wrote the best-selling book, *Beat the Dealer*, which is still considered the betting bible for all blackjack players.

With his rigorous scientific approach, he was a pioneer in this field.

To monetize his new found skill and test it in a real gambling environment, he had the genius idea to sell his betting skills to the highest bidder. He found a prospect in Manny Kimmel, business owner and notorious gambler himself with suspected links to the underworld. Kimmel offered to fund his blackjack bankroll with $100,000, but in return wanted 90% of all profits less expenses.[35]

Thorp agreed. They tested Thorp's Blackjack system in Nevada casinos. At first, the casinos he visited didn't understand why he was consistently winning. Most of them didn't try to find out. The casino managers simply made it clear that he wasn't a welcome guest anymore. Thorp knew of stories of similar good players who didn't heed their warnings. As a result, they got both their arms and legs broken in a special silent room, a room that is usually reserved for monitoring the gambling action on the floor.

Thorp decided to take his business and betting system somewhere else—Wall Street—where failure can mean many things, but never broken bones. It was the right decision. He quickly transformed from blackjack player who could win maximum $300,000 to professional hedge fund manager who, a few years later, made $6 million in fees and capital gains, from a comfortable office in California. He quickly understood that the profit potential was limitless in the hedge fund game.

Thorp applied the same betting strategy and the same money management strategy he perfected in blackjack on financial products. He only traded financial products that his mathematical calculations found to be mispriced by the markets. Early on, he recognized that warrants, (special financial contracts known as *derivatives*), were mispriced. He found their prices miscalculated and amateurish. He made a fortune for his fund, just trading warrants. When S&P futures were introduced in 1982, he traded S&P futures and made a killing. When junk bonds, were all the rage in the mid-80s, he traded those and made a killing. The explanation for this is simple: Thorp was not a gambler in a classic sense, but he had the discipline to calculate the mathematical odds of each trading idea and bet only on those that were positive. In other words, bets that were the most likely to make a profit.

It was early times on Wall Street for mathematical traders and he was able to cherry pick his bets. As soon as his competition (individual traders, other hedge funds and Wall Street institutions) caught up, Thorp moved on. His logic was simple. The moment conditions changed such that his margins fell and his risk increased (due to competition), he was out.

He noticed that with each new financial product that Wall Street actively promoted to their client, there were enormous inefficiencies. For Thorpe, their sales pitches and professional advice didn't make much sense, other than giving their clients a new way to gamble their money. But he realized, "when people invest based on useless advice, there may be an opportunity to profit." He, then, concluded that the more "naive money" was in the market, the easier it was to make money almost risk-free. For him "naive money" came from players without an edge, easy to manipulate, and with lots of money to gamble away. Wall Street nurtured the ideal market players for themselves and people like Thorp.

Bot Traders—Profits every Millisecond

Today, there is the growing group of hedge funds that use sophisticated electronic trading programs to do the trading for them. They recruit mathematicians and physicists from universities like MIT to program their trading software. They trade huge volumes of financial securities every day, and profit from small pricing inefficiencies in the market. They are not so different from traditional quant hedge funds, but they use much more computer processing power and software that trades independently from any human interference. Kenneth Griffin of Citadel is one of the leading players in this field, as is James Simons of Renaissance Technologies. Both earned almost $1.7 billion each in 2015.

Amateur and professional online poker players might have already become acquainted with bot players. Bot players are computer poker players designed to play the game of poker against humans or other computer players. They are commonly referred to as "poker bots." Computer programmers have implemented complex software, continuously developed and improved to determine the best possible strategy by analyzing the weaknesses and playing patterns of average human players. Instead of attempting to make a computer that plays like a human, they aim to play on their strength of consistency and speed over human players. This leads to strategies that can seem bizarre and are often executed at a blindingly fast rate well beyond the capacity of any human.

Bot traders are the weaponized form of these poker bots. On Wall Street, they are referred to as algo traders (algorithmic) or High-Frequency Traders (HFT). Originally, the rise of electronic trading as opposed to telephone trading, increased liquidity and speed of execution. The lengthy and at times controversial transition from human traders on exchanges to full electronic and automated trading took place between the mid-90th to the early 2000s. Ever since the rise of bot market makers used for trade execution, the electronic revolution has been praised for reducing the trading costs for all involved. However, this is not their only function.

The real revolution of electronic high-speed trading and bot traders took place between 2005 and 2007. Never too tired to make a buck, savvy bot trading hedge fund operators have found a new source of easy money-making. They allowed their bots to trade on their own accounts autonomously without any human interference. Just relying on their complex software, their processing power and sheer speed, they let their bots find the tiniest market inefficiency and place bets in lightning speed before anybody else can. Humans are betting on bot players to gamble better and faster than anyone else. Quite logically, there must be a loser, who is slower and incapable of reacting to fast market changes on the other side. It seems we do still need humans, at least for funding the few winners.

2012 data suggests that Bot trading firms accounted for 50% of all US equity trading volume. HFT firms represent 2% of the approximately 20,000 firms operating today but account for 73% of all equity trading volume.[36] The speed of trading and the sheer volume they can process each day has turned them into dominant players on all stock exchanges around the world. Their dominance will only grow with the rise of more sophisticated AI and ever-increasing processing power.

The Fat-Tail Players

Meet Mark Spitznagel, the most famous proponent of a unique Hedge Fund trading strategy and friend and former partner of

Nassim Taleb, author of *Black Swan* and *Fooled by Randomness*. He is the owner and investment manager of the multi-billion-dollar hedge fund management company Universa Investments, L.P. His investment strategy, called "fat-tail trading," specializes in *tail risk*. Tail risk is "a form of portfolio risk that arises when the possibility that an investment will move more than three standard deviations from the mean is greater than what is shown by a normal distribution."[37]

Don't worry if that made no sense to you—what it means is you develop a strategy by betting on really unlikely things—for example, being hit by lightning twice in quick succession or a meteor destroying the earth. These are freak accidents to discuss at dinner parties, but they have no relevance in normal daily lives. In almost all cases, that would be the end of it.

In financial markets, the fun has just started. Someone is going to bet on those events occurring or not, and someone is going to bet wrong. Some savvy hedge fund managers told me that it's due to the rear view mirror effect. But then again, in 2007, most people were unwilling to bet on the idea that Lehman Brothers would collapse. Some out there did, and they made a killing.

This is where Spitznagel and his funds come in. He specializes in these type of mispriced bets and makes fortunes in the process. As a result, his fund has a very peculiar return pattern. His performance pattern is almost the exact opposite of the typical mutual fund and index investor's performance pattern. The usual pattern goes like this: there are several years in a row with stable and expected returns. The average investor feels good and usually brags about his performance for a period—only to be blown out of the water with one miserable crash. Even years of satisfactory performance can be completely wiped out by one severe market correction. Many less experienced investors and traders, numb and baffled, say farewell to public market investing for several years until the next cycle repeats itself. A few hardened investors continue with the pain of falling prices to complete a horrific cycle, all the while paying annual fees for nothing.

Spitznagel is different. He is willing to lose a bit every month and for a couple of years in a row if necessary. He makes a killing in one swoop, usually resulting from one disastrous moment for financial markets. Spitznagel did this in 2008 and 2009, with a recorded performance of about 100% for his hedge fund, which doubled his billion dollar hedge fund in size. The 2010 Flash Crash was blamed on him, because he had a large bet on falling prices before the flash crash, which led him to profit disproportionately from this market anomaly. We now know that he had nothing to do with it. He simply had his regular trading positions in place. In 2015, he made another $1 billion for his investors, when markets suddenly worried about the financial conditions in China.

He calls his form of investing: "round about" investing. Though riddled with mathematical complexity, this strategy in its core is very simple. Since he only places bets on mispriced financial products, Spitznagel found a perfect niche for himself that won't be overcrowded anytime soon. Not a lot of investors are willing to lose a bit month after month only to wait for the big payout. They would rather win a bit month after month and lose a lot in one clean swoop.

All these strategies have one unifying aspect in common; *the money game* provides their lifeblood. They profit from the tiny or significant market inefficiencies this game provides, caused by an imperfect system and played by imperfect players. They thrive and feed on the masses of uninformed, slow and less sophisticated players. Without them, Wall Street wouldn't be what it is today. But it doesn't stop there. Where so much money is involved, characters that are less patient and less inclined to play by the rules are attracted. Rather than be exposed to any residual risk, all gamblers have to deal with whatever their skill level; a small group of professional players have always been on a quest to eliminate all risks, and they know how.

CHAPTER 8

———◆———

THE BIG CHEATS

"I'm scammed almost every day."
– James Altucher

As we have seen, smart investors seek an edge over others through superior and sophisticated work, better technology, a better strategy, and better information. We have seen that they make use of the same mathematical principles that professional gamblers use. As in real casinos among gamblers, there are always less morally declined players, who are not satisfied with a mere mathematical edge. It just isn't enough. Too big is the chance that money could still be lost if the vagaries of uncertainty strike at any time and will. They want the ultimate edge.

There is no better place to cheat, commit fraud, hide it under cover of sheer complexity, and receive higher incentives than in the financial markets. The most astounding reality is that most of the time, the guilty ones get away with it. For even the least informed citizen, it should be clear that financial markets are obviously places where stronger, more informed players exploit weaker players to gain an unfair advantage. As Tom Hartman claimed in *The Coming Crash*, "The industry as a whole is exploitative and corrupt." Matt Damon noted in his commencement speech at MIT 2016 that the subprime crisis "...was theft," and furthermore that "[Wall Street] knew it. It was fraud, and you knew it. And you know what else? We know that you knew it!" He would know; he was the narrator of the 2010 award-winning documentary "Inside Job" which portrayed the subprime crisis in all its dark facets.

However, what's most telling about Matt Damon's speech is how little traction it got from his audience. And this isn't surprising, because it's in the nature of the system to appropriate the very people it victimizes. For thousands of MIT graduates heading off to Wall Street to pay off their colossal student debts, the temptation to cut corners is powerful. Now imagine if you join an institution where fraud, corruption, and secrecy are a part of the culture – like Enron or BCCI. If you had the chance to make $2 million in one day, and if your bosses and colleagues all agreed that they'd cover your tracks if you broke the law– wouldn't you be tempted? For people at the top, the rewards of fraud and skulduggery can be far greater than just paying off debts.

There's no more notorious example of the temptations of financial fraud and its astronomical rewards than Bernard Lawrence "Bernie" Madoff. He was convicted of a staggering $17.2 billion dollars of fraud in 2009 and was sentenced to 150 years in jail. Once a big hot shot on Wall Street, Madoff even became the non-executive chairman of the NASDAQ stock exchange and owned his charity. He could have stayed there if he hadn't been a direct victim of the aftershocks of the subprime crisis in 2007.

In a recent jailhouse interview, he described decades of steering clear from scrutiny by regulators and "gullible customers," a phrase that he uses to refer to his former clients. According to Madoff, "Retail investors are the least well-informed market participants. The individual investor is the last person that has any information." He came to a very simple conclusion: "Scamming investors has been going on since the beginning of time, and I don't think it's going to end."[38]

This begs the questions: what popular scams are out there, and how do more informed and stronger players prey on the weak and less knowledgeable? How do you avoid being prey? It is clear that any student of investing needs to deal with these topics or they will suffer the financial consequences. In the two following chapters, I will provide an overview of some very disturbing facts and practices that any individual investor must be aware of before setting sail.

Confidence Tricks

It has been said, "Confidence tricks exploit typical human characteristics such as greed, dishonesty, vanity, opportunism, lust, compassion, credulity, irresponsibility, desperation, and naïvety." Many con artists target the elderly, misinformed, and uneducated, but even professionals and academics fall victim to confidence tricks. In financial markets, there is never a lack of "gullible" targets.

One type of con is the so-called *long con* (also known as the "long game"). A scam that unfolds over an extended period and involves a team of swindlers, as well as props, sets, costumes, and prepared lines. The purpose is simple: "To rob the victim of huge sums of money."[39]

In investing, con tricks contain most of the steps of traditional cons. There is the "Foundation Work:" the preparation in advance, including the hiring of henchmen required. Then there is "The Approach:" the victim is contacted through social media, investment boards or traditional routes (TV and door-to-door salespeople). Next is "The Build Up:" the victim is presented with a profit scheme that appeals to the victim's greed. There is even a "Pay-off or Convincer, " in which the victim takes a small payout as proof that the scheme works and that the con artist can be trusted. In a gambling con, the victim is allowed to win several small bets. In stock market cons, the victim is lured in through easy gains in the stock market, such as sure tips or IPO shares.

Finally comes "the Hurrah:" a sudden crisis or change of events forces the victim to act abruptly and usually under duress. It's a catalyst for transferring money quickly from one pocket to another pocket. In past financial markets, the Hurrah catalysts have always been market crashes, panics, sudden loss of confidence in a scheme, and most recently, *flash crashes*, "a very rapid, deep, and volatile fall in security prices occurring within an extremely short time period." Let's take a look at one of the most famous financial scams– the "Ponzi scheme."

Ponzi Schemes

The most common form of a financial market long con is the classic *Ponzi Scheme*. Named after Charles Ponzi, an Italian businessman and con artist. Ponzi schemes can be breathtaking in their scale, due to the fact that their success and failure hinge entirely on the imaginations of everyone involved.

Born in 1882 in Parma, Italy, Charles Ponzi arrived in Boston in November 1903. Financially destitute upon arrival in the U.S, he had no choice but to chase the American Dream. Early on he did several odd jobs, including dishwashing, until he got involved in a few financial scams that got him thrown behind bars twice.

Resourceful and go-getting, he finally found a legitimate investment opportunity that had elements of a simple arbitrage scheme. But, he was impatient and realized that using his own funds couldn't increase his wealth quickly enough. Always the creator of getting rich quick schemes, he needed financial leverage. The leverage would come from raising money from outside investors. To attract new investors quickly and to create his own "going viral" campaign (20th-century style), "he promised investors outrageous returns of 50 percent in 45 days, or 100 percent in 90 days."[40]

To show proof of his promises, Ponzi paid early investors returns using money from new investors, rather than with actual profits. The trick worked and soon investors stormed his office to hand over their cash. However, it went downhill from there, and most investors would never see a dime again. It might have worked out for Ponzi, had he used the remaining funds to invest in his profitable arbitrage operation and reduced return expectations. Instead, he spent the raised money lavishly, as if it were his own. According to a newspaper article: "He bought a mansion in Lexington, Massachusetts, with air conditioning and a heated swimming pool."[40]

His house of cards collapsed in August 1920, when The Boston Post investigated his miraculous gains. It set off a run on Ponzi's company, with investors losing confidence, as quickly as they had been captivated with promises of easy money. It was too late; the money was gone.

Though the original Ponzi scheme was based on fraud, nowadays they usually start with legitimate business operations. Initially, everything appears kosher, and the first profits are genuine. What follows is a typical scheme on Wall Street. An operator will artificially bump the price of a hot stock, internet startup company, or penny stock. This lures in new customers whose investments function as payoffs for people who invested earlier. Of course, con artists fill their own pockets, too. The system is self-sustaining; new investors provide money for those few investors leaving the party, but spread the good word. This is crucial—little to no value is actually being generated. The stock prices are usually horrendously overpriced and produce no real profit. The people who run the scheme gather money from one wave of investors after another, taking most of it, and passing it off enough to another set of older investors to keep them happy. The people who put in money first, usually get out soon enough to reap all their profits. Eventually, of course, the money runs out and the whole thing implodes. The most "gullible investors" in the final waves of the buying frenzy are usually the last and have the largest losses. In a way, all financial bubbles are elaborate and lengthy Ponzi schemes. If we take a closer look at the mechanics of the dotcom bubble, we would all agree with this observation.

Lasting from roughly 1997-2001, this was a period marked by the founding of several new Internet-based companies (commonly referred to as dot-coms). On one hand, the whole world was frightened by the potential of the "Y2K" bug to wreck their services, banks, and industries which had invested heavily in their IT resources. On the other hand, people believed that the Internet was the future and that nearly every single company that claimed to be a "dot-com" immediately became popular, even if it had little chance of success.

The early businesspeople who did succeed, e.g. Netscape founder James Clarke and Broadcast.com CEO Mark Cuban, made billions. These were the early adopters and winners who became the role models everyone sought to emulate. The stock prices for many businesses rose so rapidly that a global buying frenzy for all things related to the internet and technology broke out. It climaxed around March 2000, then the bubble popped. Many dotcoms disappeared as quickly as they had gotten famous. A panic broke out, and the stock market crashed; millions lost their investments, and a few even committed suicide. Those who sold early and cashed in their chips, due to foresight or sheer luck, kept their millions and billions.

One symbolic figure that stood out amongst all the successes and failures of the bubble was Frank Quattrone. He was the new poster child for greed. Quattrone helped companies such as Netscape, Cisco, and Amazon go public. At the peak of the bubble, he was earning roughly $120 million a year. In the aftermath of the dotcom bubble in 2003, he was prosecuted for interfering with a government investigation into the bank he used to work for, Credit Suisse First Boston (CSFB). CSFB came under scrutiny by federal authorities for its behavior in allocating popular IPOs to a few favored clients in exchange for inflated commissions for other banking services.

Apparently, Quattrone and his "West Coast gang" had created lucrative investment accounts loaded with the hottest and most sought after IPO stocks– stuff that would cause intense mouth-watering and fainting for any IPO hunter today. These stuffed accounts were for banking clients who became known as

"Friends of Frank." The friendships didn't end there. Once the "Friends of Frank" allocated these sure bets, they were required to pay back Quattrone with banking business– lucrative deals for Quattrone's firm. Failing to return the favor meant they were no longer Friends of Frank, and they would never see a single hot IPO share again anywhere in the U.S.

Notified of the impending investigation, he instructed his office to erase relevant documents and emails. Rather surprisingly, he never had to go to jail and all his legal fees–though substantial– were paid by CSFB in full. After the trial in 2006, he quickly claimed his overdue compensation (in the range of $100 to $500 million) that CSFB still owed him, on top of hundreds of millions more that he had stashed away. There were rumors that he was considering opening up a major charity and going into philanthropy to help orphans and widows.

Insider trading

Another form of skulduggery that every investor is aware of is insider trading, the movement of information that could have an impact on a stock's value before the information has become public knowledge.

Imagine CEO Fatcat, in whose corporation Fat Cat Inc., you own $400,000 worth of shares. He calls you in the middle of the night, because he's been caught embezzling. He's your friend, so he gives you a heads up: sell now, because in the morning, Fat Cat Inc. is going to be worth nothing. So, you sell by dawn, then sit back and watch everyone else go broke. Congratulations, you've just completed your first insider trade, and you've broken the law.

Martha Stewart comes to mind as the most prominent individual investor who got caught in the most blatant form of insider trading. In December 2001, her broker tipped her off that ImClone, a biopharmaceutical company that she had invested in, was declining in worth. It's new drug, Erbitux, had failed to get the expected Food and Drug Administration (FDA) approval. Top management and directors were informed in confidence by the authorities. Apparently, Martha's broker got wind of it as well. Stewart ordered her broker to sell ImClone as soon as possible. When the rest of the market was informed, ImClone's shares price dropped like a stone. Martha's timing was opportune, but also extremely suspicious. Was it willful insider trading, a mental blackout, or her own suffering from cognitive biases? We will never know. Naturally, she denied all charges. According to court records, she was able to save $45,673 from insider trading. Considering her net worth of $85 million that year, it was a minuscule amount. In July 2004, Martha Stewart was sentenced to five months in prison, five months of home confinement, and two years of probation for lying about a stock sale, conspiracy, and obstruction of justice.[41] Apparently, the prison sentence didn't hurt her financially. In 2015, her net worth was estimated to be north of $300 million.

Converting inside information to capital growth has always been a part of stock exchanges. The very first cases of insider trading can be traced back to the first bubbles and financial crises. In the age of Adam Smith, stockbrokers and aristocrats frequented the gentlemen's clubs. They freely traded tips and rumors and made timely purchases and sales to make more money quickly. At that time, not many people were shocked about this. It was the nature of how information traveled before modern communication.

That changed in the aftermath of the Stock Market Crash of 1929. A few people on Wall Street were able to liquidate their position early on, hence securing their wealth. But, their insider sales further depressed prices. It was an outrage for all other players, in particular for those, far from Wall Street, who learned of the crash several hours too late. As a result, Congress enacted the first insider trading laws and established the Securities and Exchange Commission (SEC) to enforce it. But obviously, it wasn't enough to control or even contain insider trading, as the following case of Raj Rajaratnam shows.

Raj Rajaratnam, founder and owner of the Galleon Hedge Fund Group, was arrested by the FBI and was found guilty of fourteen counts of conspiracy and securities fraud in October 2011. He was sentenced to 11 years in jail, which was one of the longest sentences ever given for insider dealing. Rajaratnam had developed a broad network of tipsters and business contacts who provided a steady flow of insider information. Once he was in possession of such vital information, he created an alibi for his subsequent trading actions in the form of selected research that he quickly fabricated or borrowed from numerous brokers. The case of Nortel Networks is symbolic of all of his insider trading activities. On one trading afternoon, after hanging up the phone, Rajaratnam stormed out of his glass office and called an emergency meeting with his top lieutenants. What followed was a scene right out of the movie Wall Street.

First, Rajaratnam ordered his analysts to write a research note on Nortel. In this note, they were to argue that Nortel's management hadn't shown up at a scheduled investor's conference, causing frustration and doubts among traders and investors, which would impact the entire tech sector. He, then, ordered them to send out emails to interested parties. It was the perfect justification to liquidate Galleon's heavily concentrated tech stock portfolio, and to "short" tech stocks. While his analysts were feverishly drafting these research notes, he ordered his traders to liquidate their Nortel positions and most of their portfolios.

Two minutes after the opening bell on the New York Stock Exchange, Nortel Networks reported terrible earnings and earning forecasts. During after-hours trading, their price had plummeted more than 10%, and Rajaratnam had made a killing. It was apparent that some cronies had tipped him off a couple of hours before the company released its earning news. The letter to the investors was just an alibi to justify his abrupt investment decisions.

Rajaratnam was known for pushing his employees to get "an edge" on Wall Street, to justify their high salaries and bonus payments, and he lived by his own philosophy. But, as is usually the case, his own success caused him to be complacent and sloppy in his research and trading activities. He simply didn't know when to stop, because he thought that he had a foolproof, working system. After all, it had worked for several years, by simply creating bogus research reports and alibis. But in the end, the evidence was too great for him to escape; his sloppy behavior led the FBI to bug his entire office.

Rajaratnam is a rare case because he didn't get away with it, even with the support of an army of accomplished and expensive lawyers. Steve Cohen, on the other hand, founder and manager of SAC Capital, settled all charges against him in a civil lawsuit brought forward by the SEC for failing to supervise his staff. That was, of course, after he was cleared for insider trading himself, which was entirely the doing of his minions – or, at least, that's what the final judgment was. Mathew Martoma, a former employee, was sentenced to a 9-year spell behind bars. According to prosecutors, Martoma accumulated profits of $276 million based on insider information during his time at SAC Capital. The company and Steve Cohen agreed to stop managing funds for outsiders, but paid a $1.8 billion fine, a small amount considering Cohen's overall $15 billion fortune. He is now managing his money in a family office closed to the public. Recently he has been hailed as a tremendous philanthropist for being very generous with the funds of his own family foundation, the Steven & Alexandra Cohen Foundation.

Insider trading is the true edge for a few professional investors, as it increases their odds of winning dramatically; and hence, allows them to increase the stakes and the amount of money they can place on these bets. Going to great lengths in attaining insider information is still worthwhile. The range of possible sources is endless, whether we are talking about hot IPOs, new product launches, the release of bad earnings news or any other market moving news, including spreading rumors and false reports. Insider trading will always be a gray zone, difficult to prove, and hard to track down. The official definition is already a mouthful: *Illegal insider trading refers generally to buying or selling a security, in breach of a fiduciary duty or other relationship of trust and confidence, while in possession of material, nonpublic information about the security.*[42] How on earth are you supposed to know it when you see it?

Front Running

Another technique is "front running." The textbook definition of "front running" is "the practice by market-makers of dealing on advance information provided by their brokers and investment analysts, before their clients have been given the information."[43] It simply means that a party with fiduciaries duties is in possession of order information about their client's immediate investment decisions. Hence, they can overcharge their own clients or sell this information to a third party for a cut of the trading profits. Imagine you call your broker with an order to buy 100,000 shares of Google. You want it done as soon as possible for the best price. He takes your order and calls his prop trader on another floor to buy a similar amount of Google shares. When the prop trader has completed the position, your broker buys the same amount of shares from the prop trader, with a slight price premium. Voila! Risk-free gains for the investment bank, and a perfect team play. The customer is also happy. He got his 100,000 Google's shares for slightly more than necessary, but how would he know? This is old-fashioned front running. Front running has been part of the system since Amsterdam opened its doors over 400 years ago.

However, in modern times, Wall Street took front running to a new level. In 2003, for example, New York Attorney General Eliot Spitzer began to investigate a spate of illegal late trades and suspicious market activities. After an investigation, it became apparent that some hedge and mutual funds were cooperating with each other to maximize their profits through insider trading and front running.

How was that possible?

You must understand that much market-moving news is published after the closing prices of many mutual funds are determined and announced. Those who are able to purchase these funds, at the current day closing price, after these market moving news are revealed, have a clear information advantage.

The logic behind this trade is simple: be the first in before the general market can react to news, and be the first out in the morning, when markets have time to react. On the surface, this is nothing new. In 1968, there were cases of front running and market timing investment fund prices that allowed some few chosen clients to profit from a simple information advantage. The depth and reach of this scandal in 2003 shocked even the most hardened investors. Names such as Putnam Investments, Janus, and Invesco were involved. Worse was that their behavior clearly harmed the interests of the majority of their own clients.

Alerted by Spitzer's investigations, and a bit late to the party, the Securities & Exchange Commission (SEC) launched its own investigation, which uncovered even more dubious practices among the leading mutual fund companies, which included the practice of front running in individual stock holdings rather than mutual fund prices. The SEC claimed that "certain mutual fund companies alerted favored customers or partners when one or more of a company's funds planned to buy or sell a large stock position. The partner was then in a position to trade shares of the stock in advance of the fund's trading. Since mutual funds tend to hold large positions in specific stocks, any large sales or purchases by the fund often impact the value of the stock, from which the partner could stand to benefit."[44]

To clarify this situation, imagine a huge Boston fund management company that sells or buys a medium-sized company with market capitalization between $2 and $10 billion, and distributes the purchases across all these funds at the same time. This will, inevitably, move up the stock price of the company being bought or sold, because people will see that the trade turnover has skyrocketed. Crucially, people with advanced knowledge about the fund's investment decisions could take a position in advance, usually with borrowed money to maximize gains before the fund executes its trades. Once the order flow of this big fund hits the markets and the prices increase, the same people will sell their accumulated shares to the fund with a profit.

As in the cases above, many easy and relatively risk-free gains on Wall Street rely on a simple principle that I like to call "First in, first out." If you look closely, most financial cons and Ponzi schemes work on the very same principle. The "first in" enjoy the most favorable prices, which guarantees them the easiest and biggest return potentials. What usually follows is the release of market moving new or an elaborate promotional and marketing campaign, to shift the supply and demand balance that causes prices to increase. With superior and advanced knowledge, the same operators are also the first to leave (first out), cashing out to secure their gains. Today, they might be considered "smart money."

Flash Traders

With the increase in trading speed and the rise of technology on Wall Street, we can see the new form of front running described in Michael Lewis's Flash Boys: A Wall Street Revolt. Imagine you want to purchase an ETF or single stock through your online broker. You set up your purchase order on your electronic order form close to the current market price. But somehow, whenever you hit the buy button, the price suddenly increases, making your purchase order more expensive. It's as if (cue the X-files theme) someone knew exactly what you were going to do and what your order details are. In the process, they are buying it cheaper from the market and selling it to you for a slightly higher price. That's classic front running: very small profits, but risk-free. If you multiply it by the daily billion dollar trade volumes that are traded on NYSE alone, some fantastic profits can be racked up quickly.

How is that possible? High-speed trading. Those who have access to the fastest trade execution and friendly Wall Street brokers with stuffed trading books can win over your orders and make those tiny little profits. It's simple—the trader with the fastest trading system wins and gains a tiny, risk-free profit every time.

What has been revealed by Michael Lewis's detailed accounts has caused havoc on Wall Street, with brokers, exchanges, and high-frequency traders targeted in FBI operations, and some federal investigations still ongoing. It has also revealed– again– the enormous complexity of trading systems, technology, and software involved and those few who are able to capitalize from this complexity and gray zones of regulations.

Market Manipulation

If you are a trader and your annual bonus is coming up, but the performance numbers don't look good this month, you need divine intervention. Or you could take the future into your own hands with a familiar technique called window dressing.

Window dressing is a simple form of price manipulation where you put in a large buying order at the very end of the trading day of a calendar month, and the price of that stock in question moves up a few percentage points. Who cares what happens the next day? All that counts on paper is the last price of the previous trading day, because that price determines performance numbers and bonus payments. Hence, according to one definition, "Market manipulation is a deliberate attempt to interfere with the free and fair operation of the market and create artificial, false, or misleading appearances with respect to the price of, or market for, a security, commodity or currency."[45]

In an interview with Jim Cramer with TheStreet.com, the former hedge fund manager and current host of CNBC's Mad Money, explained how he single-handedly manipulated the price of Blackberry (formerly known as Research In Motion) to his liking. These were the days when he was under pressure to make day trading profits at his hedge fund.[46] Apparently, all of his buddies were doing the same, and he admitted that he learned the trade from his wife who was by far the better trader. Ironically, Eliot Spitzer, who uncovered so many Wall Street scandals, was an early investor in Cramer's fund. Spitze decided to withdraw his funds for some election campaigns at a very inopportune moment for Cramer, nearly crashing his whole enterprise.

There are many forms of market manipulation with names like "churning," "layering," "stock bashing," or "pump and dump." I recommend remembering only one scheme, "pump and dump." Imagine that I published on my Twitter feed a new trading idea in a micro-cap (so-called "penny stocks," very illiquid and small and often dodgy companies with questionable business operations). You check the price on the trading screen of your online broker and notice that the price has gone up for the last week by more than 10%. Eager not to miss out on this lucrative opportunity, you decide to place an order for $10,000. After all, you have been following my trades on my blog and Twitter feed. The few trades I published have all been profitable. While you complete the electronic order form, the price moves up and is running away from your limit order. But damn it, now you want it even more;

and finally, your order gets filled at a much higher price. It is almost as if someone knew you were buying these stocks.

You check the price of the stock every day, and you are very pleased with the development. Your position now displays a 20% profit. And then, abruptly, I call it a day, sell all my stocks, and make a quick and easy profit of more than 30% for three weeks work. While I take victory laps in my office, open a bottle of champagne, and probably meet my buddies for cigars (and more, because I am terribly debauched), the penny stock drops like a stone. It finally trades below where it started a couple of weeks ago. Your portfolio now shows a fat, red minus of more than 20%.

You have been the sucker all along and became a victim of a semi-legal, but very unfair "pump and dump" game. It was a simple scam. I purchased stocks of a very illiquid listed company way in advance. Through my tweet and email campaign, I caused several buy orders from my loyal followers, causing the demand and supply of this particular stock to shift and the stock to rise. You just saw the end result of a covert operation that simply appealed to your own senses and the inner urge to follow up on easy gains. But as soon as I see the share price hitting my profit targets, I sell my shares to all those naive latecomers eager to grab them out of my hand at inflated prices. You might have been the last in the loop.

In the end, you decide to close the position, because you can't stand seeing the big deficit as a reminder of your gullibility. But, you swear never to trust me ever again. The following week you get an email in your mailbox that catches your attention: "How to Trade Penny Stocks for Big Profits," and the dreadful cycle repeats itself. Judging from my spam folder, this is what takes place day in and day out. As they say, "There's a sucker born every minute."

The Libor Scandal 2012

The previous example of market manipulation is nothing compared to the Libor Scandal. Libor stands for the London Interbank Offered Rate. It is connected to the well-coordinated work of a few prop desks at leading investment banks. The Libor Scandal was essentially one of price fixing. Think of the interest rate on a loan as the "price" of money. If you give me $100, and I agree to return $105 to you in three weeks, then technically, I am paying you a $5 premium for your $100. In international currency trading, this $5 premium is determined by the Libor rate. The Libor is an average interest rate calculated through submissions of fictitious rates by major banks across the world, connected to approximately $350 trillion in bonds and their respective derivatives.

On July 27, 2012, the Financial Times published an article by a former trader which stated that Libor manipulation has been common, since at least 1991. There was an immediate uproar, as the manipulation had a direct impact on many other securities traded worldwide. U.S. markets were particularly affected, as U.S. fixed income securities such as mortgages, student loans, financial derivatives and other financial products have been using the Libor rate as a reference rate for many years.

Since the scandal, academics and law firms have been trying to answer an urgent question: how much did the banks make off this? Well, so far, Barclays, UBS, and the Royal Bank of Scotland Group, all of whom were involved, agreed in 2014-15 to pay a combined $2.6 billion to resolve U.S. and European regulators' claims. Twelve global banks that have been publicly linked to the Libor rate-rigging scandal face as much as $22 billion in combined regulatory penalties and damages to investors and counterparties, according to Morgan Stanley estimates.[47]

Whatever the real economic damage was, the total penalties paid by banks are peanuts relative to the size of the entire market they have been manipulating for all those years. It is also a fact that the few bankers and traders responsible for the damage have never been prosecuted individually, while all those mutual funds, index funds, pension funds, and many more financial institutions fed the bill. I am sure that you have a real financial interest in any of those paying patsies, and all done with the money of savers and investors.

CHAPTER 9

---— ◆ —---

PUTTING IT ALL TOGETHER

"That some minority on Wall Street is getting rich by exploiting a screwed-up financial system is no longer news."
– Michael Lewis

L et me tell you a story about the early prop desks on Wall Street. Robert Rubin, Treasury Secretary under Bill Clinton and former COO of Citigroup, was part of a prop trading team at Goldman Sachs in the 70s. At that time, he worked, by today's standards, a fairly elementary trading strategy called *M&A Arbitrage* or *Risk Arbitrage*.

Imagine Company A announces that it's going to buy Company B in three months. In order to entice shareholders of B to sell their shares, company A usually offers a substantial premium to current share prices. The share price shoots up (sometimes dramatically). But there usually remains a price differential between market price and offering price, the price that the bidding company offers to shareholders of company B. This is called a spread and reflects the market's view of how likely the deal will be completed successfully. The spread can be positive or negative, depending on how likely the market considers a positive outcome. The higher the risk of a failing deal, due to regulatory or antitrust issues, the higher the spread. The spread shrinks with each passing day until the predetermined date is reached and cash flows from company A to shareholders of company B. The deal is completed and the player who traded that spread made a nice profit. It's a fantastic trading strategy if you pick the best deals and the best spreads. But it is not risk-free, as deals do get canceled, and in that case, the prices drop dramatically back to the level before the takeover bid.

This was the strategy Robert Rubin practiced and it taught him to think in probabilistic terms– a bit like a gambler calculating and assessing his odds. The interesting thing was that, at that time, Goldman Sachs wasn't that active in sourcing their own M&A deals as a traditional merchant bank. It seems that they truly aimed at avoiding any potential conflicts of interest between their own trading activities and their fee business. Goldman Sachs was still a partnership back then and required all partners to hold their private fortune against all possible losses and lawsuits. Only later did they become a global M&A powerhouse, with a giant internal hedge fund attached and a public corporate structure designed for profit maximization. They went public in 1999 in the middle of an epic tech bubble, making their partners wealthy beyond the wildest dreams of any of Goldman's founders.

Goldman Sachs is a good example of how Wall Street institutions changed and transformed themselves from the late 70s to today. In his revelations Why I Left Goldman Sachs published in October 2012, former Goldman Sachs senior trader Greg Smith describes vividly how the firm's former culture of serving the clients first turned into a culture of dog-eat-dog and bonus fetishization. Smith concludes that this cultural change is irreversible unless it is stopped from the outside. He came to the only sensible conclusion– leave the firm.[48]

If you ever ask an investment banker about a possible conflict of interest between their own trading and trading for clients, they would vehemently deny any. They would say that barriers, so-called "Chinese Walls" are in place, with trading floors separated, sometimes at different locations. Supposedly, this keeps the flow of information between the trading activities of their clients and their own trading activity strictly compartmentalized. They will also refer to ever-increasing internal compliance and risk management departments whose sole purpose it is to enforce law and order.

Obviously, this is nonsense. For starters, the senior figures within the institution have their fingers in both pies, and we are expected to believe that they never talk about business to each other. You need to understand that investment banks are a treasure chest of information. All market players have to deal with them like all gamblers have to deal with casino staff. Individual, professionals, central banks and even governments have to deal with them. Wall Street institutions are at the very top of the information food chain. Not letting the pool of information go to waste, they have been busy converting their trading floors, built to serve their clients, into profit centers that have contributed billions of net profits and created a bonus system the likes of which has never been seen before in the history of the world.

Today, prop desks resemble modern hedge funds. They operate several hedge fund strategies at the same time on different teams and for different product categories. They have very similar financial incentives with very similar risk profiles in place, and they do what they were designed to do– make money in any market conditions with the edge they enjoy. In plain English, this means to make money on the backs of weaker players. If it means treating their own clients less favorably to violate their fiduciary responsibilities and to challenge the law, so be it.

According to Greg Smith, his former top boss and Goldman CEO, Lloyd Blankfein, openly admitting to this pragmatic culture in front of a Senate subcommittee hearing. Smith is quoted as saying, "...in a sales and trading business, there is no fiduciary responsibility; that we are not obliged to do what is in the client's best interest; that we were not advising the client; that we are just there to facilitate trades between big boys (i.e., large institutional investors)."[49] If this revelation doesn't frighten you when dealing with Wall Street, I don't know what would.

But there is another part of the culture surrounding Wall Street's prop desks that is equally concerning—the world of prop desks and their intricate network and relationships with leading hedge funds. In this web of close Wall Street relationships, not only prop traders or hedge fund managers are part of it, but also a few select money managers from the largest asset management companies. But, it's the hedge fund world prop traders naturally lean towards and bond with. As a matter of fact, prop desks are the breeding grounds of new recruits for the hedge funds of the world. The very best prop managers don't go even that far, but establish their own hedge fund firms, sponsored by their banks, in which they worked for many years. Indeed, they maintain exquisite relationships with the prop desks they left behind.

Wall Street Mafia

It is a fact that there is a small community on Wall Street that knows each other personally and builds strong professional bonds. There is nothing wrong with that; nor is it illegal or immoral. But, it becomes a serious problem when a small group of people abuses their favorable positions and relationships to gain an edge over all others. With a sense of entitlement and open ruthlessness, they present themselves as invincible, which can only be considered reckless and extremely dangerous for everybody else. Machiavelli would no doubt be proud that so powerful a group seems to have taken his lessons to heart. For the rest of us, though, surely the implications are terrifying.

Some economist and industry experts trace the emergence of this openly aggressive culture and cut-throat ideology back to Enron and its notorious energy trading and deal-making teams before they went bankrupt in 2001. One trader was recorded singing, "Burn, baby, burn. That's a beautiful thing." Apparently, he couldn't contain his excitement when he made millions on the back of Californians without electricity in the summer of 2000, when a massive forest fire disrupted power supplies to California. In this chaos, Enron was able to raise electricity prices citing "demand and supply issues." It entered the history books as "the Western power crisis."

As eye-opening as Enron's case might be, there was a much more important event in financial history more than ten years earlier that provided the blueprints for Enron's trading, deal-making and accounting shenanigans. Meet Ivan Boesky and Michael Milken—the forefathers of modern investing and Wall Street.

In the midst of hairspray and the Gordon Gekkos of the 1980s, a new Reaganite ideology rose to prominence. There was no better expression of the philosophy of people like Boesky and Milken than Gekko's rant in *Wall Street* with the *"greed is good"* sermon celebrating a new age. This was based on the speech that Ivan Boesky gave to students at the UC Berkeley School of Business May 1986 commencement ceremony (Milken's alma mater).

Boesky was a hedge fund manager who traded the same trading strategy Rubin had about ten years earlier: Merger Arbitrage. But where Rubin used probabilistic mathematical models and yellow legal pads to assess the likelihood of a deal completing successfully in order to have an edge, Ivan Boesky was not as patient and mathematically inclined as Rubin. What he wanted, and based his model on, was insider information. One iconic moment that would change Boesky's life forever was his Waterloo moment with Cities Service, a huge oil company. It also exemplifies the concept of "moronic leverage," as he used sizeable amounts of his own and his wife's family fortunes.

In May 1982, T. Boone Pickens, the famous oil billionaire and former corporate raider, launched a hostile tender offer for Cities Service. The price of Cities Service shot up from around $30 to almost $60. Immediately after the hostile bid, a "white knight" emerged to rescue Cities Service from the grasp of Pickens. The white knight was Gulf Oil, which made a friendly bid at $63 a share.[50] At that moment, Boesky's trading desk got busy. He committed all his firm's capital and, on top of it, borrowed 900%

more liquidity of that from banks and brokers, totaling $70 million. He made an all-out bet on the Cities Service deal. He and his entire team were convinced it was a sure bet. According to a person involved, it was a bet "I'd put my grandmother in."[51] Their confidence was derived from a very similar takeover battle that preceded the Cities Service deal. In that deal, a bidding contest erupted between the corporate raider and the white night, generating a very handsome profit for Boesky with a very similar leveraged bet.

Unfortunately, markets don't do what you want them to do, and Boesky experienced his very own lesson of the "rear-view mirror" fallacy. On August 6th, rumors were flying that Gulf got cold feet and that the company was considering withdrawing its bid. What Boesky went through emotionally can only be imagined. If the rumors were true, then share price of Cities Service would probably plummet back to $30. At that level, Boesky's firm would have been wiped out completely. When the rumors were confirmed, the stock plunged, as expected, to $50 and then to $45 within hours. He was rescued from certain bankruptcy, thanks to a last minute miracle deal with another hedge fund manager and his close friend. And even though this deal might have saved him, his estimated loss was still $24 million, about 30% of the firm's assets. At that point, Boesky swore never to lose money again. He understood that he needed to eliminate all risk for his future bets if he wanted to remain to play the big money game on Wall Street. He needed to be at the very top of the information food chain, so he made a phone call only a week after his monumental experience. That would be one call in a series of many calls that would lead to a treasure chest of insider information about pending or failing takeover deals. When he dialed his number and someone picked up, he heard the familiar and friendly voice of a Wall Street banker.

The phone was not taken by Michael Milken or even one of this bankers. It was different Wall Street player—one of many. Both Boesky and Milken would build a unique relationship, which would make them the juggernauts of their generation. Milken represented a new breed of predator investment bankers with a "take no prisoners" philosophy. He single-handedly transformed his firm Drexel Burnham Lambert from a second-tier institution to a challenger of Morgan Stanley and Goldman Sachs for Wall Street supremacy. Ironically, Milken always disliked working on Wall Street with its old white-shoe culture and exclusive gentlemen's clubs. As soon as he got so powerful that top management couldn't deny any of his personal requests, Milken moved to Beverly Hills, California with a loyal group of ragtag bankers and traders. There, he would establish his own command center and trading floor without any operational oversight or internal controls from New York headquarters. This decision alone would seal the fate of Drexel Burnham Lambert Inc.

Milken was a genius banker: extremely hard-working, resourceful and obsessed with his work. He developed a new investment banking structure that was designed to generate cash non-stop and in amounts never before seen on Wall Street. His method was based on the two pillars of fee income and, more importantly, lucrative bets for his separate accounts. Just like Enron's Andrew Fastow had his secret accounts to book his private equity dealings hidden away from top management, Milken had his secret internal bonus account where he only booked his most profitable trades to benefit himself, his West Coast gang and his loyal followers. He developed the blueprints of modern investment banking, with prop trading desks, at the heart of the money-making machine and an elaborate network of tipsters, proxies, and henchmen. They were all generously compensated because he made offers no one could refuse. Money talks on Wall Street.

What he was capable of with this new structure could be seen at the height of his investment banking empire, when he controlled entire markets. This included the market for lucrative takeover deals financed through his innovate bond department, his crown jewel. He was regularly hired as an advisor for both sides of a takeover deal, literally negotiating with himself. He made millions in fees– advising clients, and issuing bonds that would finance all of those deals– while simultaneously trading for his account. Unfortunately, he would never see the day where his structure would unfold its full potential, where millions would be replaced by billions and entire sovereign states would give in to the power and influence of investment banks and a few hedge funds.

A notoriously impatient man, he felt he needed to speed things up. He needed someone to do the dirty work for him. Ivan Boesky fit the bill.

Milken benefitted from his relationship with Boesky through generous trading commissions, access to reliable capital sources, and the traffic Boesky's trading generated in the market. As a very public figure, Boesky even appeared on the cover of Time Magazine. Hence, Boesky had a lot of followers and piggyback investors. Most importantly, Milken was able to camouflage his trading and trade positions through Boesky's role as a secret proxy. It was a relationship made in heaven, mutually beneficial with all of the preferential treatment, kickbacks, and insider information. Unfortunately, it all came tumbling down. Milken and

Boesky wound up in jail because they were ratted out by Boesky who wore wires at several of his last encounters with Milken.

In April 1990, Milken pleaded guilty to six counts of security and tax violations. Three of them involved dealings with Ivan Boesky.[52] In the aftermath, his investment bank Drexel Burnham Lambert imploded and, by 1990, disappeared. Millions of investors lost money on a scale that was never seen before. Many of the deals that he helped source and finance buckled under the burden of very high-interest payments and a loss of confidence. As a result, it caused a wave of corporate bankruptcies and industrial consolidation, including in the US banking sector. From these ashes, giant financial institutions, e.g. Citigroup and JPMorgan Chase, emerged; they would dominate world finance for the following decades.

Milken was the real king of Wall Street at his time leaving behind the blueprints of Modern Investing and Wall Street as we know it today. As Milken demonstrated and had envisioned, the new institutions would be powered by prop desks that would dwarf anything he had ever had. With trading desks, traditional funds and hedge funds all interlinked and using state of the art technology and the best software available, a small group of astute player(s) would profit from the flow of information around the globe amassing enormous fortunes and political power in the process. Milken would not be part of this new financial order. Out of the game, and in prison, he finally tended to his charity that he had founded but had neglected during his busy career – "The Milken Family Foundation."

Why the Kamikaze?

Having studied Wall Street's money-making capabilities and some of the more dubious techniques to gain and enforce their edge, the question is: why the occasional gigantic losses? Why the suicidal missions of some financial institutions? Milken and Drexel Burnham would never reign over their financial empires. Milken got caught up in criminal charges, and Drexel collapsed under the weight of lawsuits and unfavorable market conditions that caused big bets to go bad. In 1995 the venerable old British merchant bank, Barings Bank went the way of the dodo when one employee named Nick Leeson caused massive losses through failed speculations and then tried to cover it up. LTCM blew itself up in 1998 and since the subprime crisis, everyone is aware of Wall Street's incompetence and recklessness. Its history is littered with corpses of failed investment banks and giant hedge funds. To paraphrase Michael Moore: "I think historians when they look at this time, they're going to wonder why "Wall Street" overplayed their hand like this. Why would they, when they had it so good? "[53]

Trying to answer these questions, William D. Cohan, author of *Money and Power*, made the following comment: "Why we never seem to learn from the problems caused by our ongoing reckless behavior is mysterious and unexplainable."[54]

The culprits are not alone. Even those who try to uncover the crimes and excesses of a few privileged Wall Street players are not free of their misjudgments and personal weaknesses. Elliot Spitzer, too, had to face his demons. His career nosedived soon after concluding his investigation. According to The New York Times in 2008, "Spitzer had at least seven or eight liaisons with women from a high-end prostitution agency over six months." Investigators now believe that Spitzer paid up to $80,000 for prostitutes over a period of several years while he was Attorney

General, and later as Governor.[55] Apparently, the FBI wiretapped him, alerted by suspicious money transfers under the anti-money laundering provisions of the Bank Secrecy Act and the Patriot Act. They didn't catch an international terrorist ring or financial activities that supported global terrorism. Instead, they found Wall Street's #1 enemy.

The financial theory assumes that market participants act and react rationally in the face of economic news: honestly and as intended under the law. Unfortunately, that is just an assumption. People make mistakes and give in to greed and fear. In this regard, all players and market participants – on and off Wall Street – are the same. They all tend to have their very own cognitive biases. The only difference is that some are more in control than others, and those who can, either stay away altogether or make sure that chance is as little a factor in their financial success as possible. If it weren't for a very common issue known as "overbetting," or in other words "overplaying one's hand." Wall Street would be living in a perfect world of ever increasing profits and bonus payouts.

Let me explain, one of the most common errors committed by gamblers is "overbetting." It is connected to gambler's ruin. A lot of gamblers don't know how much is too much, and they don't know when to stop. *Overbetting* is always bad and always has dire consequences – not only for the person who did the actual overbetting but anybody connected to that person. When we remind ourselves of the few failures mentioned in this book, we can trace them back to the phenomenon of overbetting by a small group of seemingly sophisticated players with or without a superior edge. It is a widely known fact that players who believe they have a clean edge over others tend to overbet regularly, especially when they bet with other people's money. But in the real world, there is never a 100% sure thing.

JP Morgan and Sea Mammals

In February 2012, some hedge funds noticed unusual trading patterns in the market for *credit default swaps* (CDS). CDS work like an insurance contract that pays out premiums, but demands full payment when a particular event occurs. These highly complex derivatives structures were the same derivatives that took center stage in the subprime mortgage crisis in 2007.

These hedge funds suspected a trader who had some deep pockets as someone who was capable of manipulating the pricing of the derivatives in question. It was later revealed that this trader was none other than Bruno Iksil, a key JPMorgan Trader nicknamed the London Whale, who was infamous for his oversized bets and willingness to take a risk and reap enormous fortunes. Apparently, he accumulated outsized credit default swaps of such a size that he moved the entire market for these products. As the London Whale, he felt invisible at times. But this time in, he clearly overplayed his hand. By the middle of 2012, other players, mostly rival banks and hedge funds, placed heavy opposing bets. Like a pack of vultures smelling blood, they collectively and simultaneously attacked the weakened target with full force. Their strategy was simple: taking the opposite side of the bet, hence squeezing Bruno Iksil out of his bet, at very unfavorable prices for him and JPMorgan. Unbelievably, this pack included another trading branch of JPMorgan that purchased the derivatives that Iksil was selling. It seems that one hand did not know what the other was doing. I suspect a more Machiavellian ideology was the reason for these inner trading conflicts on JPMorgan's trading floors. Besides, bonus time was around the corner.

As is usually the case when rumors run rampant, early reports at the beginning of 2012 were vehemently denied and downplayed by JPMorgan. In May 2012, the first confirmation came that a giant CDS derivatives position might have caused a $2 billion loss by top management. On July 13, 2012, the total loss was updated to $5.8 billion, and a spokesman for the firm claimed that projected total losses could be more than $7 billion. So from a non-existent problem at the beginning of the year, it quickly ballooned to an estimated loss of about $7 billion. Since we all know, that derivatives are the real zero-sum game, those rival banks and hedge funds had a significant payout.

On the company's emergency conference call, JPMorgan Chase's CEO Jamie Dimon said their derivatives strategy was "flawed, complex, poorly reviewed, poorly executed, and poorly monitored." Since then, the episode has been investigated by the Federal Reserve, the SEC, and the FBI. The $6 to $7 billion one-time loss might have been minor, relative to JPMorgan's large capital base of more $200 billion and $2.4 trillion in total assets at that time, but it hurt JPMorgan's price and their shareholders' performance.

And as is usually the case, experts and regulators had been asking themselves how much risk is too much, until the discussions faded out without any appropriate actions. I believe that this is a farce, and the wrong question to begin with. The real issue goes back to what risk means. If you don't know or ignore the fact of real potential losses, how can you even measure it correctly? If you leverage yourself 28 times or more, and your mathematical model spits out zero risks and you believe it, I can only say that you are totally irresponsible or completely incompetent. If you load up on financially engineered products that are as complex and devastating as creating real nuclear weapons, and you believe that society profits from these, I recommend putting a few positions in your private portfolio backed by your entire personal net worth.

Key Takeaways

Ponzi schemes, insider trading, market manipulation, and frontrunning have all been around since the emergence of the first exchanges. It's a combination of advanced knowledge, preying on the psychological fabric of "gullible" players, what we know as psychological misjudgments and cognitive biases. It gives a small group of players the ultimate edge over all others when placing their bets. In history, it has always been considered a necessary evil – an additional hidden tax on the system. However, we could argue that since the Milken/Boesky Mafia who pioneered a new culture of winner-takes-all, we have entered a new level of fraud, open aggression, and greed. It culminated in 2008 with the bankruptcy of Lehman Brothers, but it did not stop there. Insider trading, front running, and price manipulation have continued. Yet, a vast majority of other players consistently underestimate the real impact it has on their bets, their capability on assessing the future, and their odds of winning. It seems most are incapable of drawing the right conclusions... and that includes governments and their regulators.

Over the centuries public financial markets evolved and so did the games and their dominant players. The difference between the early aristocrats of the 1800s, the robber barons of about 100 years ago, and dominant market players today is that the new generation of predatory players has become more subtle, more organized, and more institutionalized. Rather than a small, but powerful group of aristocratic backgrounds or individuals with street smarts, today we deal with Ivy League MBAs, people with an average IQ north of 130, and occasionally even actual rocket scientists. They have surrounded themselves with armies of enormously capable sales and marketing individuals with questionable incentives.

Then there are the think tanks, rating agencies, law firms, and lobby activists always eager to support any quest of Wall Street might be pursuing. All professionals with high incentive payouts have mastered and honed their skills to perfection. That makes them the perfect accomplices and props to any elaborate long con, whether they are aware of it or not. The result of all this is that the few who understand how to rig the system, place big bets with other people's money, reap big profits, and their armies of minions follow. But being gamblers at heart, they never stop when they are on a winning streak; then all goes kaboom!

In the final chapter, I will discuss how to draw the right conclusions and how to take the right path in a game that doesn't leave much room for mistakes.

CHAPTER 10

————◆————

YOUR CHOICES

"A man's GOT to know his limitations."
– Harry Callahan, Magnum Force

So far, this book has described the actual nature of investing and the real risks of playing *the money game*. We have seen some side effects of a flawed financial system that is dominated by gamblers and charlatans. If a small group of gamblers takes it too far, it could jeopardize the stability of the entire financial system. They overbet and overplay their hands, and the fact that they do it on a regular basis, should be clear from this book and a personal study of Wall Street's history. From the insight you gained from the previous chapters, you should have realized that the odds of playing the money game are very much stacked against you. You must have also realized that regularly playing the money game will lead to losses and Wall Street is counting on it.

In this chapter, I will demonstrate that there are alternatives to playing the money game on Wall Street's terms and that you can still make the right decisions to build, grow, and protect your personal wealth.

Decision 1: Your First Investment

Before we go any further, let's acknowledge two simple truths about investing:

1. Any decision involving money contains risk, and hence, includes some elements of gambling.
2. Our decision-making is as much influenced by our subconscious, as it is affected by rational thinking.

The bottom line is that when making decisions about money, we always run the risk of losing it, and we are constantly influenced by powerful cognitive biases. That brings us to the first decision that we have to make about investing: what money should we use for investing, and what should be our first (and most significant) investment?

The answer is simple: you should source every investment with cash that we don't need to use in the foreseeable future. Money that isn't necessary to our daily lives. Money that is not already allocated for another future event, such as a vacation, new car, or another investment project. Hence it is a paradox– *we should aim to make money with money that we don't intend ever to consume.* There is logic in this. Any investor will find himself in hot water if he needs his money back sooner than expected. The result is substantial losses because fair prices are not able to be negotiated.

It's comparable to the situation you would find yourself in, if you needed to move to another state or country and needed cash quickly. You may have to sell all of your possessions, including your house and car, in a hurry. Under these circumstances, you would not be able to find a reasonable market price in such a short timeframe. Even worse would be if we found ourselves in the middle of a recession with generally depressed market prices for houses and cars. Thus, we can conclude that investors should use the money they don't need.

No doubt some of you will be thinking, "Yeah but I want to invest to *make* money—what's the point in investing if I already have it? And how am I supposed to get to the point where I have extra money to invest anyway?"

Your Cash Engine

The answer to the previous questions is simple: We are all, in a way, our own "cash engines," and the most valuable asset on our personal balance sheet. That is to say that we are by far our most important investment. Anybody can earn money, and if you end up spending less than you make, you have a positive cash flow. This cash inflow accumulates with each month and builds the basis of our personal wealth and future investments. But there is more to it. With each future investment you make, you should be able to increase your *free cash flow* through investment income and capital gains, reinforcing the positive cycle of income growth and wealth accumulation. It all starts with your primary cash engine.

Quite logically, it is in any investor's self-interest to make sure that this primary engine runs smoothly for an extended period, which includes living a healthy and balanced life. As corny as it may sound, your first investment should be in yourself. There is a reason why education and training is so highly valued. You can increase our own earning power through various personal investments, such as higher education, an old fashioned apprenticeship or specialized training. But make no mistake, even these investments have their risks: overpayment, failure to capitalize on skills, etc. Be that as it may, the risk is simple to assess and manageable for all. Follow the advice of Australian television presenter, Paul Clitheroe: *"Invest in yourself. Your career is the engine of your wealth."*

Decision 2: To Play, or Stay Away?

From what we now know about *the money game* and Wall Street, there are only two logical choices:

1. Stay away from the money game entirely and focus on the traditional ways of building wealth.
2. Do pretty much the same as above, but only take the best bets, with the odds in your favor, and diversify over time.

Let me elaborate on point one. The best risk management policy in the world is to not take unnecessary risks in the first place. If you don't understand the games, don't want to spend the time to learn them and don't want to let other gamblers play with your money, you eliminate risk by not participating. We always have choices and still enjoy the freedom to make our own. If your choice is to stay away from it all, don't despair. There are plenty of investment opportunities the old-fashioned way that offers adequate and, often, an even better risk-return profile with less complexity.

For example, in the past, who you shared your money with and who benefited from your earnings were intimately tied up with the ideas of family, class, and race. These social structures still exist all around the world. There is plenty of proof that countless individual entrepreneurs and family businesses have become independently wealthy without having dealt once with stock markets, fund investments, or financial markets experts, through the "traditional" route of a well-paying job or entrepreneurship. In its most extreme manifestations, large communities of the Amish (an ultra-orthodox Christian denomination) have followed this path with much success, even though they limit themselves to only a few possible professions and businesses with the total absence of technology.

What they all have in common is a simple strategy of accumulating cash and investing in opportunities relevant to them. They either continue investing in their own cash flow operations, in real estate, or keep excess cash in gold and safe liquid assets. This structure enables them to develop the right mindset: the mindset of wealthy, independent people who don't need to play the money game.

Decision 3: Speculator or Investor

So, you've decided to play the game. Great! To start, let's get something straight: there are only three ways to make adequate and consistent returns worthwhile compared to the risk you take when playing the money game:

1. You get in early and sell when interest is rising: the "First in, first out" approach.
2. You make use of great market inefficiencies that includes structural flaws and mistakes committed by others: the opportunistic approach.
3. You cheat and lie and get yourself an unfair edge: the Bernie Madoff approach.

You decide which category you want to fall into.

Next, you need to make a decision as to whether you want to become a full-time speculator or dedicated investor. As we saw in Chapter 4, investors enjoy some decisive advantages over speculators, both structural and psychological in nature. As one of my friends working on Wall Street noted: "An investor can be both speculator and investor at the same time. If a speculation doesn't work out, he can still be an investor with a long-term horizon. A full-time speculator doesn't have that luxury." As an investor, you have to make sure that you understand the underlying asset and its realistic earning potential. You want to avoid overpaying for something that might be a disappointment and could cause substantial losses when pie in the sky dreams deflate and vanish into thin air. Also, get ready for some excruciating pain of waiting for something that fits all your criteria. It surely isn't easy to reject all those promising investment ideas thrown at you over time. Very dull stretches of inactivity can test even the most patient investors when they see their cash increase month after month from their savings and existing investments. In the end, many succumb to speculation and risky bets.

To be clear, there is nothing wrong with being a speculator. As a matter of fact, many famous financial players among them Bernard Baruch, George Soros or Paul Tudor Jones II, considered themselves foremost speculators rather than investors. If you asked them why they were doing it, the answer would be because they loved it and were good at it. Their personal track records and financial successes are a testimony to their claims. But, there are many, many more who have failed miserably being speculators. Benjamin Graham himself lost fortunes betting on stock markets with leveraged bets early in his career. He had this to say about speculation: "Outright speculation is neither illegal, immoral, nor (for most people) fattening to the pocketbook."

Developing a Strategy

If you made the conscious choice of being an investor playing the money game, Graham would continue to advise the principles of any successful investment strategy:

"To enjoy a reasonable chance for continued better than average results, the investor must follow policies which are (1) inherently sound and promising, and (2) not popular on Wall Street."

Mike Burry, the famous hedge fund manager who made a fortune on betting against subprime, went one step further by emphasizing, "You have to be spectacularly unusual." Combining this with the findings from the last chapters, we can establish some fundamental principles for any investment strategy.

An investment strategy should:

- Obey the laws and principles of investing.

- Be concentrated on the investor's strengths and individual advantages.
- Be unpredictable and somewhat random– in other words, unconventional.
- Be flexible and adjustable in nature to adapt to changing market conditions.

The first principle is self-explanatory. Protection of capital and a demand for adequate returns is the simple definition of investing. Foremost, it means paying attention to underlying assets, rather than getting distracted by price fluctuations.

The second principle implies that opportunities always vary from person to person. An individual who loves tech and internet businesses may not understand opportunities in mining or health care and vice versa. Paying attention to your own strengths also has a psychological component. It contributes to that all-important "mental detachment" and the reduction of cognitive biases sneaking in. Playing home games are always easier than playing away.

The third could come right out of Sun Tzu's *Art of War*– there is never need to act conventional and predictable to any party– and that includes Wall Street. Holding your cards close to your chest is always a prudent idea.

The fourth principle about flexibility suggests that any long-lasting strategy is not set in stone, but shows elements of adaptability to changing environments and personal conditions. As John Maynard Keynes said, "When the facts change, I change my mind. What do you do, sir?" It's an antidote to the rear-view mirror fallacy that forces you to look ahead through the windshield instead of constantly looking back. When the prevailing interest rate environment is more or less zero around the world, it's only natural that the entire investment climate has changed. Hence, we need to adapt our investment strategy accordingly.

One to Rule Them All

Among professional investors, there is always a heated discussion about which strategy is best. *Value, Growth, Momentum or GARP*? It is a futile discussion and a waste of time. The best strategy is the one who ensures you don't lose money, and you get compensated adequately for the risks you take.

In a speech at the University of Southern California's Marshall School of Business, Charlie Munger further clarified this strategy:

"The wise ones bet heavily when the world offers them that opportunity. They bet big when they have the odds. And the rest of the time, they don't. It's just that simple."

Mohnish Pabrai, the famed investor and author of *The Dhandho Investor*, agreed and called it *"placing few bets, big bets, infrequent bets."* Winning the money game requires you to overcome the house advantage (i.e. all the fees, all the skulduggery, and all the predators in suits). The only way to do this is to place bets where you have a substantial edge yourself. They are rare, but they do exist. Your edge could be based on personal experience and training, financial models, pure psychology, or even better, a combination of them all. In the end, all that counts are the odds of winning and your own edge.

An Edge for the Little Guy

There is one edge we all enjoy as individual players, regardless of background or professional training. Something that is often forgotten downplayed and outright criticized as *market timing*. It is the freedom to pick the time and place of our bets. It is based on one option that we all enjoy: *the optionality of cash*. It is a permanent option that either keeps cash or invests it in any asset class within any industry at any time. In other words, we can wait for something that interests us at the right price. If nothing else is available, we have the option to say, "*No, thank you*," and wait.

You should not take this option lightly or for granted. Almost all institutional investors, including most professional asset managers, hedge funds, and prop desks, don't have that option; neither do full-time professional gamblers, day traders, and speculators. Professional money managers are paid to manage money, not to sit on piles of cash. Whenever markets rise and keep too much cash, it can seriously hurt their monthly performance. Remember, they are at least measured and judged on monthly performance. Professional hedge fund managers, traders, and prop desk traders are judged on a daily basis, so the pressure to perform is enormous. If you have chosen to become a full-time trader, you might have realized that all of those monthly subscriptions, data feeds, and memberships cost money. You are forced to meet your monthly obligations. Sitting on cash doesn't help.

Controlling our cash and cash inflows is the advantage that even the "little guy" has. Certainly, this option of keeping cash is not free and comes at a price. The foremost of these prices is the possibility of missing out and losing money.

In my opinion, the cost is negligible. This is why: We know from the phenomenon of the gambler's ruin, the tendency for gamblers to overbet and to panic on a regular basis. Mistakes are bound to happen in *the money game*. Big mistakes! It's a mathematical certainty. This offers a sure and never-ending stream of opportunities for those who can wait and have the financial resources ready. Treasure your first and most critical edge, then take advantage of it.

Finding Opportunities

Next is a matter of finding opportunities. There are two simple approaches:

1. You always search for ideas and mispriced bets in all markets and financial assets.
2. You wait until the markets offer you opportunities within your existing area of expertise.

Both are valid strategies and have their place among established and experienced investors. Many investors combine them. Full-time investors and hardened entrepreneurs favor the first approach. However, it is extremely time-consuming and requires a distinctive work ethic that can be described as "obsessive." The effort does pay off because a few talented and experienced investors find appropriate investment opportunities in almost all market conditions. This approach has one structural weakness: the practitioners themselves, their tendency to overestimate, and their skills at finding opportunities. They come up with all sorts of flawed reasoning to justify their activity and salaries, hence taking unnecessary risks.

I don't recommend this approach to the average investor, especially those who operate businesses or have everyday jobs. There is simply not enough time to show the level of dedication and commitment that this approach would require.

The second approach is much less work-intensive. You can focus on your primary cash flows—job or businesses—where you have a competitive edge and enjoy an information advantage. Only occasionally should you venture out and consider investments in either private or public markets. Of course, this only works if an investor:

1. Knows in advance what he wants to invest in.
2. Obtains a purchase price that makes economic sense, and provides plenty of safety and promises an adequate or even superior return.

Because these types of bets are rare by nature, and very different with each player, we can reject most proposals by default, especially those offered by countless third parties who have totally opposing incentives. On the other hand, if we come upon one opportunity that fulfills the criteria above, we can commit money and accept the remaining risk. After all, that is the primary job of an investor: *to take risks*.

So, start building your area of expertise. Anybody can do it. It's risk-free, and age is no limitation.

One Decision at a time

This chapter only scratched the surface of a much wider and more complex topic for developing an individualized investment strategy. I would suggest studying each topic in greater detail:

stock selection, strategy, and product categories. I have published a book on investment strategy and philosophy titled The 80/20 Investor, which is the logical sequel to this book. Also in the appendix, you will find an overview of the most relevant money games and their players. The next book in my series is a critical discussion of index funds, which are now all the rage and widely promoted. In the context of this book, I will demonstrate that index funds are just another way to keep "gullible" players in the market; and that for them, there might be some very unpleasant surprises in the making. If you have a financial interest in index funds or are considering investing and don't like surprises, this book is for you. Please register and subscribe to NomadicInvestors.com for updates on upcoming book projects.

Final Test

Here is the final test to make sure you have understood the few principles of investing and base strategy. Let's say you have $50,000 in cash and it grows with every passing month. Nervous to miss out, and eager to let your money work for you, you ask a close friend, a licensed financial advisor, and your local banker for advice. Your friend recommends a strange sounding company that has something to do with VR and AI technology, something that is popular on social media and among techies. Your banker and advisor recommend a mix of different mutual funds and ETF's that look very much alike. The banker might recommend more international stocks and your advisor higher yielding corporate bond ETFs for your mix. Tell me, what are YOUR odds of success for each recommendation? What is YOUR personal edge in any of these recommendations? If you can't answer these questions, you should remember an old poker proverb: "*If after ten minutes at the poker table you do not know who the patsy is—you're the patsy.*"

AFTERWORD

*"When the sophisticates are Accumulating, they have to
be Accumulating from someone, and when they are
Distributing, somebody has to be there to buy."*
– George Goodman

So much of what passes for investing today is, as we've seen, gambling and, we have made it respectable. It is a result of the incentive and legal structure that continues to exist on Wall Street, and that provides us with new and elaborate forms of gambles. Unfortunately, it comes with all the side effects that a traditional gambling environment attracts: cheating, fraud, and continuous streams of con tricks and Ponzi schemes. But what tops it all are the neverending losses, especially among masses of retail investors.

Wall Street counts on the gullibility of its players, and they don't disappoint. Modern capitalism seems to be powered by it. If the sacrifice is the savings and capital of masses of naive investors, so be it. As a result, there will be another massive wealth transfer to the few players who know how to play the games.

These days, the official trend is that investment banks reduce their trading operations or spin them into separate and independent legal entities and their potent hedge funds in disguise. Regardless of the regulations that continue to be imposed on investment banks, their trading operations, and their cronies will continue to survive. With the treasure chest of information they possess, easy profits and risk distribution patterns are too juicy just to give up. Their existence will reveal themselves again, when we experience another financial crisis and the finger pointing reemerges.

Even though individuals are usually responsible for any illegal actions within Wall Street institutions, it demonstrates the predominant culture. Top management at banks, of even the most reputable firms, have a "Don't ask, don't tell policy." They give conflicting signals to their troops. On one hand, they officially emphasize and enforce strict compliance rules. On the other hand, they put pressure on key personnel to come up with performance numbers to satisfy their shareholders and, more importantly, their bonus payments. A branch of Wall Street is dedicated to legally circumventing regulation in the most creative and elaborate way. When that doesn't work, the rules are bent and changed in their favor. One side effect is that a few more shady figures, don't hesitate from abusing their privileges and power positions, in manipulating even the most significant and public economic references rates to their financial advantage. This often means cheating on their competition and most valuable clients.

On the other hand, many bankers and investment professionals are ethical, hard-working, and fair to their clients. But on Wall Street, a small minority is all it takes to operate giant Ponzi schemes or bring an entire system to its knees. It took one man, Nick Leeson, to single-handedly bring down Barings Bank. It was Bernie Madoff who wiped out $18 billion of his client's assets– clients he gleefully called "gullible." On Wall Street, it only takes one person to have maximum impact.

In effect, we are all a part of a massive gamble– a big bet taken by society as a whole. We are all gamblers because we put our faith and trust in a system that is controlled and managed by gamblers who don't play by the rules, have their own financial agenda, and consistently overplay their hands. As we now know, society's bet on a bunch of gamblers could go either way. Whatever the outcome of this once-in-a-lifetime gamble, it is a colossal risk that won't have many winners.

Make Haste Slowly

The primary purpose of this book is not to pillory anybody or show that the current system is flawed, inherently corrupt, and rigged. We already know that. This book is about drawing the right conclusions for yourself and your financial well-being.

No investment will ever be without risk of losing money, not even the most sophisticated diversification model, revolutionary crypto currency or hedging techniques will change that. You don't avoid risk after you commit money, hoping that diversification or hedging will miraculously protect you from mistakes, ignorance, and losses. You avoid unnecessary risks before you make a decision.

There are valid arguments that suggest staying away from the money game altogether, and focusing only on the areas that you can invest easily in and directly control. It might be your greatest edge over Wall Street and professional players, one that even the little guy enjoys. There are also good arguments for taking a more passive role towards investing in general: you can let the market come to you rather than chase it. Always remember, you are not an institutional money manager, nor are you competing with benchmarks or other investors. Your job is not to beat indices on a weekly, monthly or yearly basis. Your single most important job is to secure your wealth, by not filling the pockets of the fat cats and other professional gamblers. Only through serious contemplation and acknowledgment of your psyche can you gain a satisfactory answer. To play or not to play? That is the question.

If I made you uncomfortable, aware, critical towards playing *the money game*, towards putting your money with Wall Street, and following conventional practice, then I have achieved my goal.

If you have realized that you are being manipulated, that you are being pushed into lousy bets for the sake of utilizing your "dormant' cash" so that others can profit from it, I have saved you a lot of money and possibly some psychological pain.

If you have realized that real wealth creation and above average returns are possible through personal investments, business ownership and taking a few, high-probability bets where you enjoy a particular edge and understand the underlying assets, you will have begun to lay down the foundation towards your financial independence and future wealth.

Similar to what Adam Smith envisioned for his utopian society of rational individuals with moral standards, the moderate self-interest of each can grow the *economic pie* for society as a whole. So study the games, practice your skills, and start investing on your terms!

Would You Like to Know More?

I am co-hosting a podcast called the 80/20 Investing Show where we discuss all matters of investing and the principles of the 80/20 investing approach. We publish a series of blog posts, investment research, and books.

I am independent researcher and self-published author. I rely heavily on my readers to continue my work. Please subscribe and become a supporter. You will have access to the free subscriber package, which includes an action list summary, a sample checklist and more freebies.

http://8020investingshow.com/support-package/

Thank You

Before you go, I'd like to say "thank you" for purchasing this book. These days we are flooded with free content and investment guides that promises the world. So a big thanks for downloading this book and reading all the way to the end. In the words of my self-publishing hero Steve Scott: "If you liked what you've read then I need your help. Please take a moment to leave a review for this book on Amazon." Let others know that this book has quality and value for readers interested in this subject.

APPENDIX I

———•◆•———

THE GAMES

Like in a casino, financial markets offer different types of games that meet a player's individual taste. Some games appeal to the masses like slot machines, and then there are games for pros with secret VIP rooms for high stakes games behind closed doors. They exist in financial markets as well. There has been a constant flow of new games. The brightest and most motivated people working on Wall Street, (with degrees in physics, mathematics, or engineering), are dreaming up new games as we speak.

In this section, I will only mention the most popular and well-established games, but the different variations are numerous and still growing.

Demand Adequate Returns

Before you start reading about the games, I would like you to spend a moment on the issue of selecting the right investment and games to play. It comes back to the option of cash: our most critical edge. At times, it might be difficult to have the exact parameters to choose the right investment. From my experience, the best and simplest filter for selecting winning investments and avoiding unnecessary risks is demanding adequate returns right from the start. Conventional textbook advice is that investors should aim for the following rule of thumb: *the higher the perceived or calculated mathematical risk, the higher the returns should be.* Tiny yields are okay, as long as the perceived risk is also minuscule. Though this is a fantastic solution for sellers of financial products because they offer abysmally low returns with generous fees, it is a far too simple guide for the world of real investment returns, unexpected events, and real losses.

Individual investors should always demand appropriate returns for any investment. Ten-year government bonds yielding negative rates or corporate bonds yielding 2% or less just don't fit the bill, even though they are considered safe in a conventional sense. Same thing with index funds that *seem* to promise 6% (and most likely much lower yields going forward), but don't even give you the promise to return your capital in full, as bonds do. Proponents of this approach, who emphasize the long-term nature of these investors, ignore the aspect of fraud, the consequences of a flawed financial system, and putting too much faith on past selective statistics.

Adequate returns might be difficult to pinpoint and might differ from investor to investor, but if we consider real business returns (returns on invested capital of the underlying assets) from various industries and historical return figures of leading investors, we can develop a sense of adequate return expectations.

From Graham's partnership records to Buffett's investment track record, we can see a return profile ranging from 10% to 20% over very extended periods of time; investing foremost in other businesses and financial market instruments without the use of excessive financial leverage. This is a return range that can be considered adequate for any conventional investment risk. If your return requirements are not met, you should keep a diversified portfolio of liquid assets, rather than commit long-term to abysmal performances and unknown risks. Remember, there are always plenty of investment opportunities in the world outside of *the money game.*

CASH—THE BASE GAME

It all starts with a simple cash flow that we can control and accumulate over time.

Without a cash flow, there won't be capital to invest. Without a constant stream of cash, we might not have the flexibility and financial perseverance to maintain a prudent investment strategy. Without continuous a cash flow, even the wealthiest investors might be forced to liquidate potentially profitable investments at the worst possible moment. Hence, if retired people think they need to gamble some of their remaining funds in financial markets, they better make sure they have a stable cash flow of existing investments or a decent part-time job. Otherwise, they might be up for some rude awakening similar to the financial crisis we saw in 2008.

So how do you establish your primary and constant cash flow? We all have one asset given from birth: time. Time can be converted into money, and it functions as a currency in life. How do you turn time into hard cash? Through work and saving, before you spend any of it. There is no easier way to convert time to cash than using our natural affinity and capacity for work. Hence, it makes sense that the first and most important investment in our life is in ourselves, through education and training.

The cash game works, and there are countless examples of individual investors with average-paying occupations or small to mid-size businesses who were able to lay the foundations of their financial freedom, even in less economically developed countries.

Yet, with all its benefits, there are two problems with this game. First, it's incredibly boring, especially for generations with short attention spans. And nowadays, it doesn't pay interest anymore. In a zero interest environment, the cash game has lost all of its remaining charms.

The other issue is that, according to financial experts and institutions, cash is "extremely dangerous" for your well-being and economic future, especially for your retirement. Apparently, the fear of inflation is so large and concern about retirement so burning hot, that they can't help but warn everybody of cash's evil nature. The message is clear: "You have to be in the markets."

Whatever Wall Street or their network of salespeople tell you, *cash should always be the preferred, default asset of choice*. Be absolutely clear: if you can't play this basic game, you shouldn't be playing any other games. If you can't earn, you have no business investing.

GOLD IN YOUR PORTFOLIO?

Gold is an excellent asset class that I love and wish that I had more. Technically, gold cannot be classified as an investment. Rather, it is *real* money that can be converted into any paper currency. It is an asset class without direct economic value creation unless you use it for industrial production or put it in your mouth as a tooth replacement. It induces high fees for brokers. Besides, you can't just walk into a convenience store, buy a Snickers chocolate bar, and pay with a bar of gold. Most of the time, if we store it somewhere securely, it costs us a substantial yearly fee to maintain the vaults and its safety/security procedures. I sometimes joke with my friends who are obsessed with it. Imagine you lay down two bars of gold, cleaned and polished, in a spacious vault where it's dark and comfy. You close the vault doors and leave it dormant for at least a year. After a year, you open the vault and outcome the same two bars of gold but with little tiny gold coins. Wouldn't that be fantastic? Unfortunately, that is just a dream.

Some consider making gold a waste of time and effort. "It doesn't do anything but sit there and look at you," according to Warren Buffett. "Gold gets dug out of the ground in Africa, or someplace. Then we melt it down, dig another hole, bury it again and pay people to stand around guarding it. It has no utility. Anyone watching from Mars would be scratching their head." When Aztec culture noticed the Spanish conquistadors' obsession with this shiny metal, they genuinely couldn't understand it. For them, it could be neither eaten nor drunk. It was useless for weapons or fabric of clothing. When the natives approached Hernan Cortes, (who invaded Mexico in 1519), on why the Spaniards had such an obsessive interest in gold, the conquistador answered:

"Because I and my companions suffer from a disease of the heart which can be cured only with gold."[59] Apparently, that disease still exists today and is stronger than ever before. Investors around the globe still buy and love gold for two reasons: wealth protection and pure speculations.

Gold Speculators and Traders

Since the early dawn of civilization, humans and societies have somehow agreed that gold is money. The choice makes sense and is not a fluke. Gold does not tarnish, can travel, is visibly valuable, and is malleable. The idea spread with its expansion over the centuries. Money can be exchanged for goods and services. It is the starting and ending point of our capitalistic system. Because there is such a widely held understanding regarding the role of gold, the market for gold is huge and relatively liquid. Countless speculators and traders are overly reliant on sophisticated trading strategies and gambling systems; have been regularly crushed by substantial market price manipulation; and, are losing substantial amounts of money in the process.

Wealth protection

For most gold lovers, it is simply an asset protection and a hedge against government induced inflation or other financial and economic uncertainties.

A person with extensive financial resources should look into purchasing physical gold at reasonable prices. Two questions come to mind:

- What are reasonable prices for gold?
- When is a reasonable time to buy gold?

First, if you have financial resources that exceed 5 to 10 times your net annual spending, there is certainly no harm in purchasing gold for the specific purpose of protecting parts of your wealth. Traditional allocations go from 5 to 10%. Anything more, and you could be considered a hoarder and rob yourself of deploying your wealth for economically sensible projects that contribute to society, such as philanthropic projects.

On the matter of price, giving a satisfactory answer is more difficult. As we have previously determined, gold cannot be valued on classic cash flow scenario nor simple demand and supply. It has its own valuation character that is often determined by psychological factors. A rule of thumb is to purchase gold whenever so-called experts predict further declines. These moments exist but are rare. In hindsight, the most obvious opportunity was in 2000 when gold traded below $300 an ounce. Another chance existed in late 2008 when it experienced a temporary decline due to supply demand imbalances. Recently, gold dropped to $1100, which in my point of view, is another reasonable entry point to build a position such as a simple portfolio hedge.

Like any asset class, there is a time when purchasing gold makes sense. In a typical periodic market crash, gold drops with any other asset class in price. There is just no liquidity in the system to make purchases possible. Wealthy independent investors with excess cash reserves and continuous cash inflows will be able to pick up gold at some great bargain prices. In the face of recent macroeconomic and geopolitical uncertainties, wealthy individuals who don't already possess gold will find that prices around even $1,300 an ounce still make sense for long-term wealth protection.

REAL ESTATE: THE ANALOG ASSET

Investing in real estate will never lose its charm as the basis of wealth creation for generations to come. However, it does come with its own set of issues and challenges that can only be managed with proper financial education, experience, and simple math.

When I was a young banking apprentice in the state bank of North Rhine-Westphalia of Western Germany, I worked for several months at the largest Builders Society in the state (Westdeutsche Landesbausparkasse). Its mission was to help millions of Germans realize their dreams as homeowners, by helping them save through a monthly savings plan at favorable savings rates. The Builders Society have been able to help customers build up the necessary home equity to apply for a traditional home mortgage with appropriate conditions. "No money down" and "teaser rates" conditions do not exist in Germany.

The savings and finance plans we sold came with all sorts of tax and government incentives. After all, Germans consider their homes their castles. Whenever money flowed from A to B, we took our cut. On top of that, with the monthly cash inflow from reliable and eager Germans, my bank was able to do more with the money that accumulated in our accounts—cash that was entrusted to us.

In the end, we fulfilled an important function within the economy and helped realize dreams of homeownership for the vast majority of our clients (mainly working and middle-class families). Even though we took our cuts whenever we could, it was still a true win-win situation for everybody involved. But not everyone will treat you with as much respect because pitfalls can range from overpaying to outright fraud.

House Flipping

In the U.S, the whole process of financing and encouraging people to buy their own homes, even when they can't afford it, has become a nightmare. During the years leading up to the subprime crisis of 2007 and even after that, the term "house flipping" or "real estate flipping" became popular among the masses of amateur investors and professionals alike, all the way up to Wall Street itself. It is a type of real estate investment, in which "an investor purchases properties with the goal of reselling them for a profit. Profit is generated either through the price appreciation that occurs as a result of a hot housing market and/or from renovations and capital improvements." As is usually the case with such booms, the smell of easy and quick money led to a gold rush of unseen proportions. Very soon, house maids and delivery boys owned 4 to 5 properties, "flipping" themselves to new riches of wealth, only to end up with less than they had started. House flipping in general, like speculation, is nothing illegal, or even immoral in the strictest sense. However, if an entire population or group of amateur investors join the fun, and the financial incentives to cheat, fraud, and abuse the uneducated public are high and barely kept in check, the entire economy and society have a problem. Even today, eight years after the crisis, the world is still digesting its effects.

Real Estate for Investment Purposes

Real estate with a conservative down payment and proper finance plan, purchased at moderate prices, makes economic sense. It is a fantastic asset on anybody's balance sheet. But, it's an asset that costs money. Don't make the mistake of thinking of your home as an investment. According to Robert Kiyosaki, author of the Rich Dad book series, buying the first house you live in is not an investment in the strictest sense of the definition. It's either shelter or liquidity, not both.

Real estate, as an investment, is probably one of the easiest assets to value, but it has its own circumstantial challenges. Consider the traditional Japanese middle class during the asset bubble years between 1986 to 1990. During the period when Japan experienced its own epic stock market and real estate bubble in the late 80s. The Japanese Imperial Palace and its adjacent land (3.41 km^2 or 1.32 m^2) were considered more valuable than the value of all of the real estate in the state of California.[56] A generation of middle-class families saw themselves in a severe economic dilemma. On one hand, middle-class families had well-paying jobs where the unemployment rate was extremely low, and the economy was booming with experts projecting an ever more prosperous future for Japan. On the other hand, real estate for ordinary folks was simply too expensive relative to their already generous salaries.

As in any industrial society, property ownership is a strong symbol of wealth and social standing. An entire generation felt that it had no choice other than to buy properties for their families, regardless of the cost. Those who couldn't afford to live in the center of Tokyo were ready to endure 2 hour daily commutes just to secure their dreams of having their own homes.

Their decision to buy homes at any cost had some very eye-opening, long-term consequences. More than 20 years since the bubble popped in Japan, I interviewed some of the families who had decided to buy homes at the peak of the bubble. The picture they described was, depressing yet revealing.

Those who could afford houses and apartments in central Tokyo were all sitting on huge book losses if they ever decided to sell. Those who were able to buy somewhat cheaper properties outside of Tokyo, with an average commuting time of one hour, were in an even more dire situation. Land prices have gradually declined, and the value of their homes has steadily written down. Houses in Japan are only built to last 30 years, and the Japanese population growth has been declining since the early 2000s. As a result, general demand will only decline.

Many owners, bound to their properties, feel as if they have no choice but to finish their mortgage and continue living where they are. Most of them learned bitter lessons, but still prefer to keep their hard earned cash in hand or in zero interest-paying bank accounts.

Lessons Learnt

Leaving some of these extreme cases aside, property ownership teaches aspiring investors all of the essential elements of prudent investing: the time involved, the detailed work necessary, and the fees paid to third parties. Investors learn about real estate taxes and the regional economic development, by managing appropriate return expectations and assessing financial risk prudently. Most importantly, it will keep the majority of middle-class families out of casinos.

People who have developed a bigger risk and entrepreneurial appetite could buy their first real estate for investment purposes. The most important financial guideline would be to purchase at a price that makes sense relative to the "expected cash flow," all relative and built on conservative assumptions. Don't forget any repairs or additional investments that you would need to do to enhance the value of the property, as determined by increased cash flow potential. There is a lot more to managing a real estate investment well than just the location.

BONDS: WHEN TRUST IS TRADED

The international bonds market is huge. In 2015, it was estimated that the global bond market was about $100 trillion large, with the United States having the largest market, followed by Japan.[57] These markets are played foremost by professional players, such as pension funds, insurance companies, large bond funds, and financial institutions. Bonds are less important to individuals unless they are incredibly rich and can stand the boring nature of bonds.

Bonds are also called fixed-income securities, because their contractual obligation is to pay out fixed interest, a coupon at a predetermined time, to the holder of these securities, usually semi-annually. They are also obliged to return the nominal amount in full at the end of the contract— usually between 3 to 5 years for corporate bonds and much longer periods (e.g. 10 to 30 years) for government bonds. The primary function of bonds is to raise funds to be used for business projects like establishing factories, developing new products, or even financing M&A activities. For governments, a bond's main functions are to fund government projects (including wars) and to finance their budget deficits. Bond issuance can influence world economies and financial markets. They represent the building blocks for many other financial products, including currency trading, interest rates swap trading, and other complicated derivatives structures called structured notes, that will be discussed under derivatives.

Trading Bonds

The important point readers should understand and remember about bonds and bond markets is the importance of *bond price fluctuations*. A solid economic idea that attempts to raise funds from the public to finance significant economic and social projects, bond price volatility have become a breeding ground for all sorts of gambling, side bets, and fee income sources for the facilitators.

Let me explain; if a bank loans you money to buy a house, that's it. Both parties know what to expect and what to do. The contract can be securely saved in respective vaults and not be touched again until the contracts expire.

Somehow, people decided to trade using these papers and with each other even though the contractual obligations between the person who issued these securities and the current holder of these papers didn't change at all. Just imagine your mortgage bank provided you the original mortgage and decided to sell your mortgage contract to another buyer. It might have decided it didn't want to be your mortgage bank anymore, or just wanted to make a quick profit due to the price fluctuations of your original mortgage contract. Maybe, it just wanted to do more business and generate more fee income by issuing new mortgages with the money it received from the sale. All is well, but then the next buyer decides to sell again or create new financial products on the back of the original mortgage (which is entirely possible with modern financial alchemy). You can see how the long chain of people owing each other can lead to confusion and errors.

Bonds are like classic bank loans contracts: just for large corporations, institutions, and governments, but standardized so that the owner of these securities in question can change with a push of a button. Their active trading creates liquidity for markets and the ability to raise more capital. There are many kinds of variations of bonds that investors can buy and trade today, such as high yield bonds (junk bonds), TIPS, zero coupon, and convertible bonds. Because bonds are influenced by daily interest rate fluctuations that move with any economic news, there is a lot of trading action going on in the bond market on any given day or time. The most popular and most liquid bonds are sovereign bonds of leading economies such as the U.S., Germany, or Japan.

EQUITIES: GAMBLING WITH OWNERSHIPS

Everybody knows, of the stock market its dramatic crashes, vast fortunes, and suicides. Wall Street—market ticker tapes flickering along big screens and Bulls and Bears- – is the graphic image that comes to mind when we talk about stocks and equity markets.

The theoretical concept behind stocks is that each represents a contract that entitles the buyer to buy equity in a public company. It is simply entering into part ownership of a company that is listed on a public stock exchange. It's like a bar of chocolate where one piece of it is broken off and handed to you as your share of the bar. The rest of the chocolate bar is divided up among the remaining chocolate lovers.

With your share of the company, you are entitled to dividends payments, if any (i.e. a proportion of any profits, in the form of annual or semiannual payments). Shareholders usually have voting rights at annual shareholder meetings where they can vote on matters of significant corporate policy. Another wonderful advantage of owning shares is that you could never be sued personally for what is going on within the company, as your losses are limited to the value of the piece of contract you own. Unfortunately, when a company does go belly up, shareholders are the last to see anything from a liquidation auction. Banks and bondholders have the preferential right to be served first. Like any investment category, there are different forms and types of shares, but the above description sums up the largest portion of the market. Other than that, there is not much else to know about simple stock contracts.

The Mechanics

To buy a share of a publicly listed company, you need to open a brokerage account to access the stock exchange. An individual can't just go to a stock exchange directly and say, "I want to buy ten shares of IBM." You need a proxy for that. That would be your stockbroker. In other words, your stockbroker is your facilitator to trading financial products on regulated exchanges. Today, all of them have online trading capabilities that reduced the cost of trading enormously. Nevertheless, making use of proxies is not free. Brokers, through their expensive licenses to access stock exchanges, execute client's orders, and place their newly acquired shares into a separate account at a depot bank (a particular bank that specializes just as trust bank for safekeeping) under your name. Make sure they do that and don't lend your shares to anybody else—contact your broker for that.

The days of easy profits for brokers, of making money through trading commissions, and of market makers are long over. When I traded my first stocks, I paid 1% commission of my invested money on both sides. Today, through an online broker, you might pay less than $20 per trade.

Nevertheless, the industry has found other ways to earn money. What they lost on percentage commission, they made up for in the sheer trading volumes of today's markets. Active Fund managers, including hedge funds and the ever-increasing group of day traders, secure a constant flow of profitable business for brokers. It's only logical that brokers have a very real pecuniary interest to keep up this flow, and even increase it over time—at all costs.

Not so long ago, you were able to get these beautiful stock certificates that looked like oversized bills. A good friend of mine who worked in the industry got me an old stock certificate from a now defunct Japanese Brokerage House called Yamaichi Securities, which was one of the largest securities firms in Japan. Today, this worthless piece of paper is framed and still hangs in my room where I grew up. In the age of electronic trading systems and the internet, most financial transactions have become paperless. Why should traders get a stock certificate when most buyers sell their shares in seconds or minutes later in a frantic day of trading activities? It looks great, with all the Japanese characters, important looking seals, and long numbers at the bottom and back of the certificate. That gift is also a reminder that, especially in stock markets, nothing is forever.

DERIVATIVES: HYDRA WITH MANY HEADS

I wish I could save you from studying this topic. It is complex and goes beyond any 101 class on investing. In fact, it is reserved for only the most serious gamblers and financial professionals—and perhaps lawmakers. But because these products in aggregate have become the largest market that has ever existed, we need to be aware of these instruments. I will try to be as brief and as entertaining as one can be when writing about financial WMDs.

According to the Bank for International Settlements, the global derivatives market is now $1.2 quadrillion or $1,200 trillion. Compare this to the entire global equity market, which was estimated at US$69 trillion at the end of 2014. It represents less than 5% of the derivative's market pie.

Standard derivatives have been around for decades and are highly regulated. It is a controlled but leveraged, a side bet on other games such as stocks, bonds, and commodities. There are financial futures, forwards, options, warrants, etc. All simple forms of derivatives based on these broad asset classes are traded on exchanges or in private transactions over the counter (OTC). The most common and oldest forms of financial derivatives are commodity products such as corn, rice, or wheat. Farmers, who were unsure of their commodity prices at the end of a farming season, were able to fix their prices in advance, hence avoiding any negative price surprises in the future. They could still lose money if prices rose higher than they had expected, but they were able to plan ahead. For this kind of trade to function, a counterparty was necessary to guarantee these prices. These were the gamblers who speculated on either falling or rising prices. They were vital for this system to work.

According to Investopedia's definition: "A derivative is a security with a price that is dependent upon or derived from one or more underlying assets." But, the real cunning aspects of derivative contracts is that it introduces the factor of short-time periods and leverage to the equation, making derivatives much more complicated and suitable for gambling and betting on all possible future outcomes.

When we consider the classic underlying instruments of standard derivatives, such as stocks, bonds or commodities, the element of time plays a secondary role. In the case of stocks, there aren't any time limits at all. Derivatives, however, include the aspect of financial options. They deal with much shorter periods. They contain the elements of financial leverage, as these products are purchased at a fraction of their actual contract size. Academia has published groundbreaking research on how to price these standard derivative products, and they have become part of any international stock exchange. But when we talk about modern derivatives, those that can be considered financial Weapons of Mass Destructions (WMDs) are a different kind of bread—a more evolved beast.

The real innovation and magic of financial derivatives rose to the surface when a few clever investment bankers started experimenting and combining standard derivatives with aspects of several other financial securities. It probably all started with the mortgage bonds department, headed by Lew Ranieri of Salomon Brothers, who has been credited with developing a multi-trillion-dollar debt-securitization market that transformed the face of finance. Everything from mortgages to car and credit card loans to purchases from banks could be sliced into pieces, repackaged, combined with other financial products, and then sold to investors around the world. From then on, it was possible to create all sorts of new cash flow payout scenarios, when an underlying base financial product moved. A new, more potent, form of side bets was created. In many cases, sides bets on the first layer of side bets and so on. Increased financial leverage grew exponentially as each layer of a side bet was just one intentionally created side-effect.

Like in a chemical laboratory where some mad scientists in white lab coats performed gene mutations and cross-breeding, new financial products were created by combining simple bond cash flow structures or simple interest rate structures (interest rate swaps) with the character of optionality and massive financial leverage. Different types of cash flows were engineered together, and a new breed of giant financial securities emerged with some fascinating results.

Because we are not talking about principal investments, only imaginary cash flow payments far into the future, we can say that they add a huge swoosh of financial leverage into the mix. If you pay for derivatives contracts, you usually only pay for just a portion of the entire nominal derivative contract, arguing that if cash flows are imaginary and dependent on uncertain outcomes in the distant future, why should I pay now for the entire contract?

Fair enough, in today's markets, most participants trade derivatives with each other, while only a tiny fraction of the full nominal value of the structure are paid and settled for. Let's say the nominal value of a contract is $1 million. Professional participants would have deposit just a fraction of this, for instance, $50,000, as collateral. Attached with the promise that if anything goes wrong, you will pay it later and settle the difference. The existing spirit among financial institutions is "Don't worry; I have the money somewhere—I am good for it." Over the years, insurance companies, governments, and even the largest hedge funds, joined the party, such as previously mentioned LTCM.

The real beauty of this financial innovation is that it is not only a combination of standard derivatives products with different forms of future cash flows, but it also has an opaque and complex nature of individually negotiated super contracts. As soon as financial regulators and rating agencies gave their green light, it was henceforth possible to trade these newly engineered financial instruments. They were traded between trading departments of investment banks, their largest institutional clients, and sophisticated professional investors in private transactions over the counter (OTC)—hidden far away from the public, regulators, shareholders, and sometimes even their own top management.

Why do These WMDs exist?

The official textbook explanation for their existence is that derivative structures provide vital liquidity to all financial markets, and provide insurances (hedges-protection) against a wide range of risks that investors face on a daily basis.

So why do they exist? It's very simple; they represent fantastic win-win opportunities for anybody who deals with them, except for the taxpayer who might pay the bill at the end of each boom and bust cycle that financial markets a prone to experience.

Derivatives structures are the perfect fee-generating product for financial institutions.

"Modern derivatives products are excellent fee generators, bet with other people's money and collect high margin fees on both sides of each transaction." One investment banker once told me that as a general rule, the more exotic and complex they are, the more financial institutions can charge for them. They can make very generous commissions on huge volumes that are just mind-boggling to anyone who has never seen Wall Street salaries and bonus payments.

It's perfect for players of these products, too, of whom there are many. Because there are so many market participants trying to hedge all possible risks, there are plenty of gambles available for players who are willing to take the opposite side of the trade. For anyone who wants to hedge risks or simply transfer risk, someone on the other side must be willing to take on this risk. These are usually players with a much bigger risk appetite or want to collect risk premiums that function almost as insurance premiums at insurance companies. This group can satisfy its urge to bet on a wide range of possible future outcomes. The derivatives markets also come with a giant market of auxiliary services attached, ranging from information, research and pricing technology companies to catering to all of the possible needs that risk hedgers or risk takers might have.

Derivatives and Society

The textbook explanations for complex derivative products and their markets might still be acceptable for society as a whole. After all, we have already gotten used to legalized gambling.

Unfortunately, these financial instruments are part of real industries and real economies. From ordinary commercial banking handing out consumer and student loans, to traditional investment banks at the heart of any functioning economy is normal. Because they are so incredibly complex and gargantuan in size, any mistake could cause a chain reaction similar to what we experienced from 2007 to 2009.

The real cost of derivatives

What textbooks and academic research simply ignore is the cost of fraud and other illegal activities that necessarily are a byproduct of any financial product and market. Recent history has repeatedly proven that any motivated party that wants to hide losses or manipulate international capital markets has found the ideal instruments to do so. It ranges from simple fraud with Orange County's state finances, to more elaborate schemes that included Enron, Long Term Capital Management, and Greece's fudging of budget data to get into the Euro. What is the real economic long-term damage for entire nations and today's incredibly interlinked world economies? Nobody knows, but we will certainly find out in the next financial crisis that inevitably is bound to happen.

Let's take a look at our final game category, a game that has become so attractive that, in the hearts of the biggest Wall Street players, it ranks second only to derivatives products: Funds, the lovable game of money pools.

FUNDS: THE CONDUITS

Have you ever met a person who got rich through investing in standard mutual funds or index funds? I haven't. You will certainly never see stories with young smiling couples leaning on sports cars in front of large mansions, with subtitles like, "We made millions with mutual funds" or "How to get rich with mutual funds in 30 years—almost risk-free."

On the contrary, I have met many people who got incredibly rich managing funds and providing fund products and advice to clients of funds. Whenever money flows, they scoop up their fees. It's obvious from a business perspective that the main incentives managing other people's money lie in increasing their assets under management (AUM) to improve their fee income.

Funds are investment products that people invest in different asset classes and have various investment strategies and philosophies depending on who's managing them. They only differ in contract details, individual terms, and conditions. Mutual funds, exchange-traded funds and even hedge funds are included in this category. As a whole, they present a giant slice of global financial markets. The mutual fund's industry alone controlled $23 trillion globally in 2011, with Blackrock managing over $4.7 trillion for clients.[58] For retail investors, it provides exposure to global financial markets and a sense of how the big players on Wall Street play their games. On the other end of the client spectrum, it allows institutional investors to have their vast financial resources managed by third party fund management companies.

Any fund represents a pool of money that charges management fees to those who manage operational expenses, such as salaries for staff, offices, and budgets for research sources, technology, and software. Clients can buy them at banks, through the internet, in private placements or on public stock exchanges. It is only reasonable to assume to read the fine print for each fund product. Nevertheless, they all promote themselves as diversification tools that allow individuals to participate in many different asset classes and financial securities around the world. This is something impossible with a $50,000 portfolio.

If you look closer at their holdings kept at any point of time, they very much look alike. Depending on their fund and asset category, they all invest in the same things at the same time. It's a known fact that fund managers copy each other. They go to the same conferences and watch the same TV channels and read the same research. Sometimes you might read or hear that a fund outperformed its competitors because it was "overweight" in tech stocks, which simply means it had a slightly larger position in Google or Apple Inc. (or some other similar) shares in their portfolio than the rest.

Completing the spectrum of third party asset managers, I would like to add venture capital and private equity funds. Venture capital provides early-stage capital for startups and promising technologies until they cash out when companies go public in IPOs or sell to other strategic investors. At the other end of the spectrum are private equity funds that restructure businesses and entire industries. In the process, they take ailing, publicly listed businesses private, restructure them and sell them at a profit by either selling them to strategic investors or relisting them on public stock exchanges. In a bull market, these listings have the same effect as start-up companies doing IPOs. They generate huge profits for private equity firms, which are lucky enough to ride bull markets. At the very end of the lifecycle spectrum, we have special funds that only focus on distressed assets or companies. That could be non-performing loans at banks, distressed real estate portfolios or purchasing the remaining caucus of businesses that declared bankruptcies to squeeze out the remaining money which might be left over. When Lehman Brothers declared bankruptcy in 2008, it was a feast for these type of investment funds. They scoured over the dead body to find any jewel that might have been hidden in giant portfolios of toxic sub-prime market assets.

APPENDIX II

———•◆•———

THE PLAYERS

The players that participate in Wall Street's money game can be divided into two broad groups. On your right-hand side, there is an army of retail, individual, and slow-moving institutional investors. On your left-hand side, you have your smart money or those players who have an edge or create one for themselves. Prop desks and a few select hedge funds with the right connection on Wall Street belong to this group. It's only natural to assume that they are all in it for the money, and they all want to win. But they all can't be winners.

Each group can be subdivided into several subgroups. This is where I would like to introduce the most significant and noteworthy players to orient you to the world of finance.

RETAIL INVESTORS: THE VERY BOTTOM

By far, the largest group in terms of sheer numbers are retail investors. They have average jobs, but they feel very strongly about being involved in financial markets and investing in stocks or funds—they want to play *the money game*. They invest either through their 401k, IRA, or online brokers. Since governments and public companies have been pushing the defined, contribution schemes like the 401k in the U.S., many individuals find it necessary to study the basics (at least) about fund investing and financial markets.[59]

Among them is a growing number of DIY investors and traders. They spend countless hours after work and on weekends studying the market or considering quitting their boring day jobs and becoming full-time traders. They are lured in by popular books and trading courses, which promises easy profits and excitement. I compare them to the growing number of full-time poker players. Yes, some of them make huge amounts of money. But, being up on top requires constant playing and honing their skills. The performance curve is, of course, skewed to the extreme. Only a small percentage makes the majority of the trading profit. The rest provide liquidity and money to the few winners and operators.

In reality, amateur traders compete against armies of professional traders bankrolled by investment banks and hedge funds. As a beginner, you will always be regarded and treated as the very bottom of the Wall Street food chain. "Dump money," "cattle," "zombie herds," "sheep," and "Muppets" are the many expressions that professionals use to describe that crowd. To be fair, they don't use these terms on retail investors, but also on large and less sophisticated institutional investors.

For brokers, advisors, or private bankers, the average retail client represents peanuts; so, it is not worth spending much time on them. That's why Wall Street has been working on standardized procedures and packages to serve this group in the most mechanical and efficient manner. Promises are for individualized, and customized services go right out the window.

It is simple economics. Your average 20k or even 50k portfolio does nothing to move the needle for a financial institution and their advisors unless it is packaged into larger money pools (funds, the conduits). Everybody knows that an email auto-responder is much more efficient at communicating with the customer individually. The same stands for computer voices on telephone hotlines. The lower the human interaction between client and financial institutions and the lower the cost per customer, the higher the potential net profits become. According to Reuters, "Facebook's Zuckerberg has opened up its Messenger app to developers to create chatbots, hoping that by simulating one-on-one conversations between users and companies, it will expand its reach in customer service and enterprise transactions." We will certainly hear more of "fin-tech" or "robo-advisors" in coming years.

SUPER RICH: THE CONNOISSEURS

Among professionals, the super rich are referred to as Ultra High Net Worth Individuals (UHNWI). They usually have their private bankers in Switzerland and even have their own family office where their sole mission is to manage their money affairs. According to Investopedia, "A person with investable assets of at least US$30 million, excluding personal assets and property such as one's primary residence, collectibles, and consumer durables. Ultra High Net Worth Individuals (UHNWIs) comprise the richest people in the world and control a disproportionate amount of global wealth."

UHNWIs are catered to by the top of the crop of private banking and financial services industry. Whether they need help with their inheritance, estate planning, new family trust, or structure of their tax declarations, they get advised by the best of the best. If they want access to new pre-IPO shares from brokers, placement of new hot funds, or invite to exclusive events, they will usually get their wish fulfilled. Like all clever investors, they want to be the "first in, first out" players. Of course, their private bankers and advisors listen for a generous compensation.

UHNWIs are not without their weaknesses and faults. Like any investor, they can become victims of their extreme insecurities. They are exposed to smooth talking, private bankers and their advisors who are interested in maximizing their fees. When bubbles reign on entire economies, they too are captivated by it. Otherwise, they quickly see themselves becoming unpopular in their exclusive circle of the ultra-rich.

On top of that, they have to constantly battle family disputes and the set of very unique challenges that comes along when one has too much money. It can consume their private lives with fatal consequences.

It is important to note that very few UHNWIs have become rich through financial market investing (maybe hedge fund owners). Almost all of them acquired their wealth by having established ownership in operating businesses or through their inheritance. From my personal network, I have rarely met or heard of UHNWI clients amassing new fortunes with stock or fund investing. On the contrary, like anybody else, they have been losing money. It seems that even with preferential treatment by the elite, private banking professionals investment success is not guaranteed.

This begs the question—wouldn't it be easier to focus on the primary money-makers and businesses, and keep a simple, conservative cash and investment strategy?

INSTITUTIONAL INVESTORS: THE ELEPHANTS

The largest investors in town regarding assets under management (AUM) are institutional investors. They include pension, endowment, and insurance funds. The biggest pension fund in the world is the Government Pension Investment Fund (GPIF) of Japan that has about $1.1 trillion assets under management and employs more than thirty third-party asset managers. Only a few years ago, the GPIF decided to diversify parts of its holdings into international bonds and global equities, away from its ultra-conservative policy of only investing in domestic government bonds and other fixed income securities.

These types of investors are big and slow-moving. They have many institutional constraints and underlie strict regulation and supervision. They are managed by investment committees and have strict fiduciary duties towards their investors. They have a few structural disadvantages over individual investors or hedge funds, but can move markets and are a force to be reckoned with. They are the elephants at any party. But due to their size and, at times, inefficient management structures, money gets lost through attrition, such as overpriced third-party consultancies, investment management, incompetence in the face of market crisis, and self-aggrandizing operators at the top.

ASSET MANAGERS: A BUSINESS MADE IN HEAVEN

Because institutional investor's assets under management (AUM) are so large, they delegate some, if not most, of their investment management responsibilities to third-party asset managers. Famous asset managers include PIMCO, Wellington, Janus Capital, and BlackRock. They are the second-largest group of institutional players on Wall Street that readers will either compete with or join as customers.

Asset managers manage a broad range of separate funds that include mutual funds, exchange-traded funds, index funds and even hedge funds—anything that can generate a fee and increase their own assets under management. They are mostly well-run businesses, and their business is size. Whether actively or passively managed, they are paid based on how much money they manage, rather than on how well they manage it. This especially counts for index funds.

Friends with Benefits

The vast majority of fund managers disappoint in generating performance for clients; index fund managers don't even try. Their funds look alike and follow the same standard formulas of modern portfolio management. Active managers still believe that they can outsmart each other. On top of this, they always struggle with clients withdrawing funds abruptly and unexpectedly, forcing them to liquidate lucrative positions, a phenomenon that is known as "forced seller."

From my experiences, these industry challenges don't cause most fund managers sleepless nights, fretting over average performance, or beating the competition by 0.5%. After all, their salaries are de facto guaranteed and paid for in advance. There might be some variances in their bonus payments depending on general market performance, but they won't have to line up at a soup kitchen anytime soon.

They enjoy some additional perks and benefits. Most of their clients are not aware or at least suppress it as well as they can. By pooling money into large funds, and in effect having complete power over those funds, fund managers, and their companies enjoy all sorts of benefits that are covered-up, flashy prospectus and long disclaimers. There has been a lot of lip service given when it comes to the topic of fiduciary duties. However, there is this massive gray zone that a lot of people will not touch with a six-foot pole. As we have seen from previous chapters, both brokers and fund management work in close cooperation together. Over several decades, they have created mutually beneficial relationships. I have been a part of this whole industry and have seen some of the inner workings and mechanisms of Wall Street's darker underbelly. I saw how brokers sold their research to institutional and professional investors when I worked on the side of the research broker. Additionally, I saw how brokers garnered hedge fund clients when I set up my own hedge fund operations, and I became a customer of their research and trading services. I surely didn't pay for all of those excellent dinners and nights out with brokers. I would be lying if I told you that I didn't enjoy it, or didn't have a good time. But, that is a topic for another book.

CENTRAL BANKS: THE FAILING MAGICIANS

The biggest manipulators in today's market are most certainly central banks.

Central banks around the world are crucial for the entire financial system. They provide liquidity and control monetary policy through the control of interest rates and other complex financial tools. The central bank's interest rate policy has become the ultimate cost of opportunity because they represent the default return rate for sovereign debt obligations. The Federal Reserve of the U.S. is the world's most influential of central banks because it controls the USD, the reserve currency of the world. All commodities are traded in USD, and most of the world's debt is traded in USD.

Current Issues

All the main central banks around the world have been struggling to stimulate the movement of money in our economic system. In the simplest of terms, their goal has been to boost the flow of money within our financial system that banks lend to institutional clients and retail customers alike. They, then, use the money to invest or consume, stimulating our economy as measured by GDP. It is called velocity of money, and central banks have been feverishly trying to kick start its revival. Obviously, without much success. Banks, corporations, and consumers suffered from the hangover of the last financial crisis. The vast majority has simply become more cautious with the usage of money out of concern for the future. That pre-eminent attitude among the major market players is poison for central banks and their mission to do their jobs. Let's see what other desperate measures they'll pull out of their rabbit hats to get us to spend and invest our money.

GLOSSARY

Assets Under Management (AUM): Is the total market value of assets that an investment company or financial institution manages on behalf of investors.

Black Swan Event: An event that comes as a surprise, has a major effect, and is often inappropriately rationalized after the fact with the benefit of hindsight. Nassim Taleb who popularized the term regards almost all major scientific discoveries, historical events, and artistic accomplishments as "black swans"—undirected and unpredicted. He gives the rise of the Internet, the personal computer, World War I, dissolution of the Soviet Union, and the September 2001 attacks as examples of black swan events.

Cash Engine: An engine that produces cash non-stop as long as it runs. Anybody can earn money, and if you end up spending less than you make, you have a positive cash flow. You are yourself your primary cash engine—take good care of it.

Credit Default Swaps (CDS): CDS are complicated financial contracts. They work like insurance contracts paying out premiums to the holder but demanding payment in full when a certain event occurs to the seller.

Chinese Walls: An insurmountable barrier, especially to the passage of information. Wall Street firms use these barriers to block information flowing from one department to another, usually in the form of access key restrictions or separate office locations.

Flash Crash: The quick drop and recovery in securities prices usually caused by computer glitches, flawed programming or order manipulation.

Financial Leverage: Refers to the use of debt to acquire additional assets. A lot of traders borrow money to magnify small speculation gains.

First in First out Principle: A strategy to be the first of any investment fad, bubble or market hype and sell before anybody else can, reaping the first and easiest gains, while latecomers provide the necessary liquidity to exit smoothly.

Force Majeure: Unforeseeable circumstances that prevent someone from fulfilling a contract.

Free Cash Flow: Equals net income + depreciation charges minus any capital investments and money needed to maintain operations at current levels.

Fund of Funds (FOF): Funds that invest in other funds managed by other companies or different fund managers. It not only spreads the risk of each diversified fund but also among different fund strategies or asset classes. Of course, all this risk diversification comes at a price in the form of another layer of management fees for the managers of the Fund of Funds.

Gambler's Ruin: Refers to a phenomenon where "a gambler who raises his bet to a fixed fraction of bankroll when he wins, but does not reduce it when he loses, will eventually go broke, even if he has a positive expected value on each bet."

GARP Investing: The GARP strategy is a combination of both value and growth investing. It looks for companies that are somewhat undervalued and have solid sustainable growth potential. Garp stands for Growth At a Reasonable Price.

Hostile Tender Offer: Is the acquisition of one company (called the target company) by another (called the acquirer) by directly asking the shareholders directly rather than negotiating with the target's management. To be successful, the acquirer needs to convince a large percentage of shareholders to get the acquisition approved.

House flipping: Is a form of speculation on real estate properties and their market prices. By purchasing property, which is expected to rise in value due to demand and supply changes or property improvements, buyers can make a quick profit but only if the speculation pays off. As soon as they've realized a certain profit, they move on, selling their property in order to deploy their cash in the next speculation.

Intraday: Intraday refers to price movements of a given security over the course of one day of trading.

Investor's Itch: An investor's psychological weakness to have the urge to be active, because they think they might lose out or miss some exciting action.

Liquidation Value: Liquidation value is the likely price of an asset received through an open market sale. Liquidation value is typically lower than fair market value. The money you would get through liquidating your entire asset column at short notice is an investor's base valuation model.

Long Con (also known as the "long game"): This a scam that unfolds over an extended period of time and involve a team of swindlers, as well as props, sets, costumes, and prepared lines. The purpose is simple: "to rob the victim of huge sums of money."

Market Capitalization: Is the market value of a listed company derived from multiplying its total number of shares outstanding with the current market price.

Optionality of Cash: Is a permanent option that holder's of cash possess, to either keep cash or to invests it in any asset class, within any industry at any time of the holder's liking and personal preference. Institutional investors including most hedge funds and private equity funds don't have that option.

Overpayment Risk: The most important risk definition for retail investors. It is the risk of paying too much for an investment target than the real value you receive in return. Overpayment usually leads to deferred losses.

Prop Desks: are places where 'prop trading' takes place. Prop Trading stands for proprietary trading—industry jargon for "trading with your own money instead of your clients."

Quant Hedge Funds: A sophisticated and complex hedge fund trading strategy using quantitative analysis and computer-based models in order to calculate the mathematical odds of each bet versus the invested capital necessary, while aiming to reduce the statistical form of risk.

Return on Capital (ROC) or return on invested capital (ROIC): Is a ratio used in finance, valuation, and accounting, as a measure of the profitability and value-creating potential of companies after taking into account the amount of initial capital invested.

Risk Arbitrage (M&A Arbitrage): Is an investment or trading strategy often associated with hedge funds. Two principal types of merger are possible: a cash merger and a stock merger. In a cash merger, an acquirer proposes to purchase the shares of the target for a certain price in cash.
Going Short: Selling something in advance, in the hopes that you buy it back at a lower price in the future.

Tail risk: A rare form of portfolio risk that—"The possibility that an investment will move more than three standard deviations from the mean is greater than what is shown by a normal distribution."

Time value of money: Refers to money concept that the importance of cash in your hand is much more valuable than the same amount of cash in an uncertain future.

Ultra High Net Worth Individuals (UHNWI): A person with investable assets of at least US$30 million, excluding personal assets and property such as one's primary residence, collectibles, and consumer durables. UHNWIs comprise the richest people in the world and control a disproportionate amount of global wealth.

Yen Carry Trade: A currency trading strategy in which traders borrow a low-cost currency like the yen and buy high-growth currency, netting a profit. In recent years, for example, Japanese housewives began accumulating Australian dollar deposits, which yielded a significantly higher rate than they could get at home."

White Knight: A person or company making an acceptable counter-offer for a company facing a hostile takeover bid.

Window Dressing: A simple form of price manipulation. Usually, refers to the market price manipulation on the last trading day of a calendar month in order to raise the prices of key holdings in a portfolio. The purpose is to make monthly performance figures more appealing to existing and new investors.

ACKNOWLEDGEMENTS

I would like to thank my launch team and all the people who reviewed and critiqued this book. Special thanks to my editorial team. My editor, Subodhana Wijeyeratne, has been a great help and guidance in formulating some general arguments on a complex topic. His wealth of historical knowledge has been extremely helpful in identifying some of the trends discussed here. I would also be remiss in not mentioning the tireless efforts of Valerie Smith as critical voice and eye of the team. Both are very talented writers, whom I highly recommend. I would like to thank my numerous friends from the DC community, as well as my sources and contacts in the financial industry, who have always offered a helping hand and their personal views. As always, I am grateful to my parents. Only due to their selflessness, have I had numerous and very much cherished opportunities.

GET IN TOUCH WITH THE AUTHOR

Twitter
https://twitter.com/WooSchneider
LinkedIn
https://jp.linkedin.com/in/WooSchneider
E-mail
info@thewritingale.com

MORE FROM THE AUTHOR

THE 80/20 INVESTOR: Investing in an Uncertain and Complex World

Are you ready to set yourself free?" The 80/20 Investor, harnessing the power of the 80/20 principle, simplifies investing. In no time, you will learn where to look for "no-brainer" opportunities, find out how to finance your investment opportunities and minimize risks. This book allows you enter the seemingly intimidating world of investing, with valuable tips from some of those who have changed the game– The Rothschilds, Hetty Green, J. Paul Getty, Henry Singleton, and others. Only with financial freedom can you live the life you want to lead. Let The 80/20 Investor show you the way.

AVAILABLE ON AMAZON

INDEX FUNDS & ETFS: What they are and how to use them

Index Funds and ETFs have seen stratospheric growth since the collapse of 2008 – benefitting from computerized trading and quantitative forms of investment management. No matter where you look, the gospel of index fund investing has been taken to heart by the media, and the masses, alike. For the mass consumer, apparently, this form of "passive investing" is far superior – even revolutionary.

But what is the truth? How exactly do index funds work? Are they really the sure bet they're made out to be? This book will offer a different perspective – one that takes into account the history, structuring, and theorizing behind index funds and ETFs, and lay bare the inner working of the industry. Beginning with the ideology underlying these new darlings of the financial world, Index Funds and ETFs will take you through a journey, exploring what indices are; how they are formulated; the legally tenuous relationship between indices and the funds that track them; the flaws in the logic underlying many investment plans; and finally, a detailed plan how to make the most out of these products.

<u>AVAILABLE ON AMAZON</u>

NOTES

[1] Amazon.com (2016). Retrieved from:
https://www.amazon.com/gp/bestsellers/
books/10020675011/ref=pd_zg_hrsr_b_1_4_last

FOREWORD

[2] La Roche, Julia (2016). Warren Buffett's right-hand man gave a dark warning about American finance. Retrieved from
http://www.businessinsider.com/charlie-munger-warns-about-american-finance-2016-4

[3] Damon, Matt (2016). Massachusetts Institute of Technology (MIT) Commencement address June 2016.

CHAPTER 1

[4] Investopedia. Investing 101: What Is Investing?. Retrieved from
http://www.investopedia.com/university/beginner/beginner1.asp

[5] Graham, Benjamin (2006). The intelligent investor: the definitive book on value investing. New York, NY: HarperCollins Publishing, Inc., p. 79.

CHAPTER 3

[6] Harari, Yuval Noah. Sapiens: A Brief History of Humankind (p. 27). HarperCollins. Kindle Edition.

[7] Farrow, Paul (2012). Fidelity China Special Situations fund manager Anthony Bolton has been shanghaied in China. Retrieved from
http://www.telegraph.co.uk/finance/personalfinance/investing/9217436/Fidelity-

China-Special-Situations-fund-manager-Anthony-Bolton-has-been-shanghaied-in-China.html

[8] Wikipedia. Black swan theory. Retrieved from https://en.wikipedia.org/wiki/Black_swan_theory

[9] Jorion, Philippe (1999). The Story of Long-Term Capital Management. Retrieved from http://www.investmentreview.com/print-archives/winter-1999/the-story-of-long-term-capital-management-752/

CHAPTER 4

[10] Keynes, John Maynard (1936). The General Theory of Employment, Interest and Money (Chapter 12)

[11] Smith, Adam (1976). The Money Game (Kindle Location 53). Open Road Media. Kindle Edition.

[12] Investopedia. Wall Street Definition. Retrieved from http://www.investopedia.com/terms/w/wallstreet.asp

[13] Wikipedia. Gambling. Retrieved from https://en.wikipedia.org/wiki/Gambling

[14] Bernstein, Peter L. (August 31, 1998). Against the Gods: The Remarkable Story of Risk. Wiley.

[15] Wikipedia. Gambler's Ruin. Retrieved from https://en.wikipedia.org/wiki/Gambler%27s_ruin

[16] Bernstein, Peter L. (1998). Against the Gods: The Remarkable Story of Risk (p. 14). Wiley.

[17] History of probability—Wikipedia, the free encyclopedia. (n.d.). Retrieved from https://en.wikipedia.org/wiki/History_of_probability

[18] Wikipedia. Stochastic. Retrieved from https://en.wikipedia.org/wiki/Stochastic

CHAPTER 5

[19] Godin, Seth (April 26, 2011), Linchpin: Are You Indispensable? Paperback

[20] Macdonald, Toby (2014). How do we really make decisions? Retrieved from http://www.bbc.com/news/science-environment-26258662

[21] For a complete list of possible human misjudgments, I highly suggest to study and research the list included in "Seeking Wisdom: From Darwin to Munger, 3rd Edition" by Peter Bevelin. An excellent book that contains many more cognitive biases relevant to money management and investing.

[22] Munger, Charlie (1995). Speech entitled Psychology of Human Misjudgement. Harvard University.

[23] Chatzky, Jean (2015). Why women are better investors than men. Retrieved from http://fortune.com/2015/04/10/why-women-are-better-investors-than-men/

[24] Pilling, David (2009). Japan's fearless women speculators. Retrieved from https://next.ft.com/content/6c1a6eb2-fc8b-11dd-aed8-000077b07658

CHAPTER 6

[25] Marriage, Madison (2016). 86% of active equity funds underperform. Retrieved from https://next.ft.com/content/e555d83a-ed28-11e5-888e-2eadd5fbc4a4

[26] Arjun, Kharpal (2015). Deutsche Bank to shed 35,000 jobs, exit 10 countries. Retrieved from http://www.cnbc.com/2015/10/29/deutsche-bank-reports-q3-net-loss-of-60b-euros-barclays-h1-pre-tax-profit-398b.html

[27] Gara, Antoine (2016). Compensation At Goldman Sachs Rises 5% Even As Profits Tumble 71%. Retrieved from http://www.forbes.com/sites/antoinegara/2016/01/20/compensation-at-goldman-sachs-rises-5-even-as-profits-tumble-71/#12d803537c92

[28] Nakamura, Yuji (2016). The Tokyo Whale Is Quietly Buying Up Huge Stakes in Japan Inc. Retrieved from http://www.bloomberg.com/news/articles/2016-04-24/the-tokyo-whale-is-quietly-buying-up-huge-stakes-in-japan-inc

[29] Lynch, Peter (April 3, 2000). One Up On Wall Street: How To Use What You Already Know To Make Money In The Market – Simon & Schuster Paperback, p. 242.

[30] Ponzio, Joel (2009). F Wall Street: Joe Ponzio's No-Nonsense Approach to Value Investing For the Rest of Us. Adams Media, p. 13.

[31] Ponzio, Joel (2009). F Wall Street: Joe Ponzio's No-Nonsense Approach to Value Investing For the Rest of Us. Adams Media, p. 17.

CHAPTER 7

[32] Gabelli, Mario J (2000).The History of Hedge Funds—The Millionaire's Club. Retrieved from http://www.gabelli.com/news/mario-hedge_102500.html

[33] Poundstone, William (2006). Fortune's Formula (p. 172). Hill and Wang. Kindle Edition.

[34] Poundstone, William (2006). Fortune's Formula (p. 82). Hill and Wang. Kindle Edition.

[35] Poundstone, William (2006). Fortune's Formula (2669). Hill and Wang. Kindle Edition.

[36] Lati, Rob (2009). The Real Story of Trading Software Espionage, AdvancedTrading.com,

[37] Investopedia, What is 'Tail Risk'. Retrieved from http://www.investopedia.com/terms/t/tailrisk.asp

CHAPTER 8

[38] Patel, Sital S. (2013). Madoff: Don't let Wall Street scam you, like I did. Retrieved from http://www.marketwatch.com/story/madoff-dont-let-wall-street-scam-you-like-i-did-2013-06-05?page=2

[39] Wikipedia. Confidence Trick. Retrieved from https://en.wikipedia.org/wiki/Confidence_trick

[40] Bio. Charles Ponzi Biography. Retrieved from http://www.biography.com/people/charles-ponzi-20650909#early-scams

[41] Hays, Constance L. (July 2004). Martha Stewart's Sentence: The Overview. Retrieved from http://www.nytimes.com/2004/07/17/business/martha-stewart-s-sentence-overview-5-months-jail-stewart-vows-ll-be-back.html?_r=0

[42] U.S. Securities and Exchange Commission. Retrieved from https://www.sec.gov/answers/insider.htm

[43] Concise Oxford English Dictionary

[44] Wikipedia. 2003 mutual fund scandal. Retrieved from https://en.wikipedia.org/wiki/2003_mutual_fund_scandal#cite_note-2

[45] Wikipedia. Market Manipulation. Retrieved from https://en.wikipedia.org/wiki/Market_manipulation

[46] Task, Aaron, Executive Editor, The Street.com. Interview with James Cramer. Wall St. Confidential: Cramer on Games Hedge Funds Play

[47] Masters, Brooke (2012). Banks' Libor costs may hit $22bn. Retrieved from https://next.ft.com/content/0231ace4-cc1d-11e1-839a-00144feabdc0

CHAPTER 9

[48] Smith, Greg (2012). Why I Left Goldman Sachs: A Wall Street Story (Kindle Locations 2917-2919). Grand Central Publishing. Kindle Edition.

[49] Smith, Greg (2012). Why I Left Goldman Sachs: A Wall Street Story. Grand Central Publishing. Kindle Edition.

[50] Stewart, James B. Den of Thieves (p. 101). Simon & Schuster. Kindle Edition.

[51] Stewart, James B. Den of Thieves (p. 105). Simon & Schuster. Kindle Edition.

[52] Paltrow, Scot J. (1990). Sobbing Milken Pleads Guilty to Six Felonies. Retrieved from http://articles.latimes.com/1990-04-25/news/mn-322_1_michael-milken

[53] Michael Moore (2011), "I think historians when they look at this time, they're going to wonder why the wealthy overplayed their hand like this". His comments during an appearance on MSNBC's.

[54] William D. Cohan. Money and Power (2012). Knopf Doubleday Publishing Group. Kindle Edition.

[55] CBSNews (2008).Spitzer Spent Up To $80,000 On Call Girls. Retrieved from http://www.cbsnews.com/news/spitzer-spent-up-to-80000-on-call-girls/

APPENDIX I

[56] Haeber, Jonathon (2007). Japan's Palace Grounds Once More Valuable than California. Retrieved from http://www.cbsnews.com/news/japans-palace-grounds-once-more-valuable-than-california/

[57] Chappatta, Brian (2016). The $100 Trillion Bond Market's Got Bigger Concerns Than Brexit. Retrieved from http://www.bloomberg.com/news/articles/2016-06-26/the-100-trillion-bond-market-s-got-bigger-concerns-than-brexit

[58] Karr, Robert (2016). BlackRock Is Expected to See Growth from ETFs and Active Business. Retrieved from http://marketrealist.com/2016/06/blackrock-is-expected-to-see-growth-from-etfs-and-active-business/

APPENDIX II

[59] López de Gómara, Francisco (1943). Historia de la Conquista de Mexico, vol. 1, ed. D. Joaquin Ramirez Cabañes (Mexico City: Editorial Pedro Robredo, p. 106).

GLOSSARY

Source: Wikipedia and Investopedia, available under a Creative Commons Attribution-Noncommercial license.

Made in the USA
Lexington, KY
09 November 2017